IMPROVING RESULTS
FROM BUSINESS ENTERTAINING

Improving Results
from Business
ENTERTAINING

How to get what you want over lunch

Melvyn Greene

**Kogan
Page**

First published by M.G. Publications 1984

Cartoons by Ray Raymonde

Republished in 1986 by Kogan Page Limited,
120 Pentonville Road, London N1 9JN

British Library Cataloguing in Publication Data
Greene, Melvyn
    Improving results from business entertaining.
    1. Business entertaining
    I. Title
    659.2   HD59

    ISBN 1-85091-164-9
    ISBN 1-85091-162-2 Pbk

Printed in Great Britain by
Biddles Ltd, Guildford and King's Lynn

To Helen
For all the early years I travelled without you,
and to all the future years we will travel more
together.

About the Author

Melvyn Greene has specialised as a management consultant in the hotel and food service industries since 1961. He is well known in Britain, Continental Europe and by many major American groups, particularly those with hotels outside America. He has worked for almost every British hotel group quoted on the London Stock Exchange and his firm's services cover the full range from hotel feasibility studies, marketing reports, food concepts, design and planning of food and beverage operations. He now specialises in advising companies on strategy, and introducing Willing Buyers to Willing Sellers, usually on large hotel deals.

He is a Fellow of the Institute of Chartered Accountants, a Fellow of the Hotel, Catering and Institutional Management Association, a member of the Institute of Marketing, and a Founder Fellow of the Tourism Society. He is a well known public speaker on the subject of marketing trends in the hotel and food service industries. He has travelled extensively in his work and is very experienced in business entertaining. He is the author of two management and marketing books and a series of short booklets listed below.

Management Books
Improving Hotel Profitability (Northwood Publications)
Marketing Hotels into the 90s (William Heinemann)

Smaller Booklets:
Improving Hotel and Catering Sales
Plan to Succeed
Planning for Change
Redefining Marketing Goals
Plan to Succeed in the Eighties
Increasing In-House Sales
The Rising Cost of Subsidised Catering

Preface

Business entertaining can be a valuable management tool. Better techniques in this important area can make a major impact on goodwill, help the successful close of contracts, and increase sales generally.

Many executives plan other sales situations very carefully. Considerable thought is given prior to placing an advertisement or sending out a mailing shot. But often business entertaining just happens! There is a strong case for planning business entertaining as a sales tool in the same way as other sales techniques, i.e. when, where, how often.

In everyone's marketing and sales action plans, a certain number of days should be set aside in advance, in order to entertain key customers – in addition to the entertaining which arises as part of normal business activities.

A successful business lunch is unlikely to be the sole reason for obtaining an order. But done badly, executive entertaining can lose business. Done well, it can move a sales situation forward and give that all important edge over competitors who do not entertain at all, or who do it in the wrong way, without the thought and planning outlined in this book.

This book is about doing it the right way and giving you that edge.

Contents

Acknowledgements

Many people helped me with the research for this book. In particular, I would like to thank Miles Quest, Managing Director of Wordsmith & Company who edited the book, Elizabeth Gadsby, Director of the Hotel Catering & Institutional Management Association who criticised it constructively, and Desmond Parte, partner in Stoy Hayward & Co. who assisted with the chapter on tax implications of entertaining expenses. Last but not least, Dorothy Woff who typed and retyped the manuscript.

1

Introduction

Very few businessmen find business entertaining extremely pleasurable. In most cases a working lunch means that the business executive hardly gets any break from work throughout the day.

Many people talk sarcastically about three hour business luncheons but my experience is that the vast majority of them are work. Businessmen work primarily by using their brains and communicating (talking). I have known three hour business luncheons which have been as exhausting as any lengthy meeting round a boardroom table.

Even American Presidents have scorned the so-called 'three Martini business lunch'. In my experience it is a minute proportion of businessmen who actually see the business lunch as an opportunity to have quite a few drinks. Rather, most executives I know look upon it as a good opportunity to do business.

Business entertaining is a unique opportunity to get together with a buyer or prospective buyer, in a personal way which is virtually impossible during business hours. It is also an invaluable opportunity to 'research' the prospective buyer and get to know him (and his organisation) better. You can ask many more questions over lunch than at a meeting in an office.

About a year ago I had a call from a friend who is managing director of a major leisure and travel company. He said he wanted to 'pick my brains'. He had to do some important business entertaining in the Heathrow Airport area. He knew the restaurants, and the hotels with restaurants, around the airport, but which to choose?

Rather than give him a quick reply, we started to go through a list of questions and points until the decision on where to go to eat was obvious. In effect, I had prepared the first outline checklist of key points set out in Chapter 3.

About the same time, I met a London-based 'rising' executive whose company was negotiating a major contract with a prospective buyer from the North. The purchaser arrived at King's Cross, was picked up by a car, taken to the offices and they started negotiating at around 11.00 a.m. The sales situation went very successfully and at 12.45 p.m. they decided to break for lunch. It was suggested that the young executive should take the potential buyer to lunch and they would continue the discussion afterwards.

At the point when they were saying 'See you again around 2.30 p.m. after lunch', everything was going fine. The young executive booked at the most expensive restaurant near their office but something went wrong during the luncheon. The executive told me he could not understand what could possibly have happened. During the meal he kept stressing the main advantages of the deal from the purchaser's point of view and there seemed no reason why he should have 'gone cold' on him during that particular period of 1½ hours.

When they arrived back at the office after lunch, everybody sensed that the buyer was far less receptive to their sales message than he was prior to lunch. About an hour later the buyer suddenly said that he had just remembered there was an earlier train. He left around 4.00 p.m. and the contract went to a competitor.

The young executive said he thought he had done something wrong during the meal period and we decided to work through it and check the things he had done right, and the things he had done wrong. The reasons why this young executive and his colleagues went wrong, will become apparent in Chapters 3 and 4. One major reason was that they should *not* have delegated the luncheon to a young member of their team.

In a sense, these conversations led to the writing of this book as

I find that some executives are worried about this particular aspect of selling.

At an early stage I decided that what was needed was *not* an extensive book on this subject but one which a busy executive could read in around three hours and then, if necessary, re-read, and a book that was written in checklist form.

In your business career you have to negotiate and sell much of the time. In fact, there is an argument that even if you are not directly involved in selling, most people spend virtually all of their time in some kind of negotiation and selling, even if it is just selling themselves.

Selling can involve paid advertising, unpaid media publicity, telephone selling, mailing shots and sales letters. It usually involves a considerable amount of face to face selling. The sales situation may be in your own office or factory or in your clients'/customers' offices and premises.

However successful an executive is nowadays, most realise that they must continuously strive to improve results in all kinds of sales situations. If you want to improve results you can learn from empathy, experience and a degree of constructive self criticism.

It is no exaggeration to say that there are hundreds of books on selling and on various sales techniques. There are dozens of courses to help you improve sales results, ranging from short intense road show type courses, which often last about half a day, to more extensive courses on marketing and selling. But there is one important sales situation for which little training is ever given and which appears to be totally neglected. This is one of the most sensitive make or break situations, namely, business entertaining in its various forms, hence this book.

After deciding to write this book, I spent a lot of time talking and interviewing people on the topic. During my research I spent more time talking to executives who are being entertained, rather than those who entertain, because it is important to understand both points of view. More time was spent talking to people who could be *your* clients and customers, than talking to the person entertaining, although virtually everyone I met did both. I was trying to use empathy to write from the opposite view to the person entertaining. I also used my own experience of entertaining and being entertained and two decades of knowledge in working in the hotel and restaurant industry.

During my interviews with many executives, I thought initially that this book would be purchased by young executives, and useful for more experienced executives. In fact, many mature executives I spoke to said that they would find the book invaluable because it is really only over the last ten years that business entertaining has been used much more as an important sales tool.

The names of specific restaurants are not mentioned for a variety of reasons. As described in Chapter 3, I use three restaurants regularly when I entertain. *All* are good restaurants. But I have never used one for business entertaining over dinner because it has an ambiance which is good for *social* entertaining but not appropriate for business. Another one has widely spaced tables and is ideal for private discussions. Women executives seem to prefer the decor and menu of another. So I use the one most appropriate to the circumstances. Two are restaurants within hotels.

But your own circumstances and customers will be different to mine, and you must choose your own venues. If I mentioned the names of restaurants I prefer, then this book would turn into a guide and this is not the intention.

The object is to help you increase your sales by improving your results from business entertaining, not to recommend specific restaurants by name. This could have major disadvantages because a year or two may pass from the time of writing this book to the time it is read. In that period the restaurant ownership may change, the chef could leave, or the whole menu and concept could change.

Some restaurants and organisations are mentioned to illustrate a point. At no time are any of the criticisms of restaurants or organisations generally, meant to refer to any named in later chapters.

A few executives who entertain on business tell me that they are not 'selling' and some said they dislike the word! Even if you are, for example, a banker and do not feel you are selling, then I am sure you will agree that you are sustaining or creating goodwill. If so, the book is written for you.

Some organisations have 'customers' for their products or services and others have 'clients'. The hotel industry has 'guests'. Please forgive the use of all three.

The key points in each section are numbered for ease of reference. I would urge you to discuss and argue about the various points with your colleagues, in order to improve your own technique and results on business entertaining. Numbered points should help in this direction.

There are no references on the correct (or so-called correct) wines to drink with what food, nor is there an explanation of haute cuisine. I am assuming that business executives know something about wines and in any case, there are many books on wine and good food. This book is about helping to move forward a business relationship, and a sales situation.

2

Pre-Planning and Empathy

Selling will never be successful unless there is a high degree of pre-planning and thought before the actual sales situation. Often people go wrong because they do not allow sufficient thought and time for pre-planning before selling begins.

Successful selling when entertaining on business, requires the same amount of research, pre-planning and thought as any other sales situation, and in many cases more so – particularly as you are selling generally away from your own office. You will see a constant emphasis throughout on the need for research and pre-planning.

The other vital point is the use of EMPATHY. Everyone involved in selling knows this is the ability to put yourself in the other person's shoes so that you can work out what is motivating him to buy, whether he is interested, whether he is a decision maker. In business entertaining it is important to be able to put yourself in the other man's seat in order to decide whether you should keep quiet and let him talk, whether you should keep quiet because he is eating, and when is the key time to start making sales points during the meal.

Not all of the points made are relevant to every set of circumstances. It is up to you to choose the key points in the following chapters and checklists, which are most relevant. The situation will vary depending on whether:

(a) you have never met before and you have never entertained him.

(b) you have met before but have not entertained him to date.

(c) you have met many times before but entertained infrequently.

(d) you have met and entertained many times in the past.

Obviously, particular care has to be taken with (a), (b) and (c) and most of the key points on the following chapters are applicable. The last situation should be more relaxed.

It could be that the business entertaining is during a long day's negotiation, or you have just met for lunch (or dinner). In other situations, you may be dining together at the end of a deal when negotiations have been completed. This is a kind of celebratory situation which is really the only one where you can relax the strict self control recommended on the consumption of alcohol.

Particular care has to be taken in (a) and (b) where you have not entertained before and this book has a greater emphasis on these more delicate situations.

Female Executives
The situation will also vary depending on whether you are entertaining a woman executive or she is entertaining you, a common occurrence nowadays. Chapter 5 is included for female and male executives entertaining women. I would like to apologise to women executives for the constant use of the masculine in this book – it is just impossible to include 'he' and 'she' in every set of circumstances.

Some feminists have argued with me that it is wrong to have a separate chapter for female executives in this book. They argue that the circumstances are identical and there should be chapters for *all* executives, not a special one for women. Virtually all the points made in the next two chapters are applicable to both men and women. But female executives who are beginning to entertain more and more on business, experience some problems which men do not. This justifies a special chapter to be read in conjunction with the rest of the book.

Empathy tells you that a first-time visitor to a restaurant experiences a 'threshold barrier'. He is entering a 'strange cave' for the first time. This could mean that this buyer, or potential buyer, may feel slightly unsure, slightly more tense and therefore less receptive to your sales approach. Some even become annoyed, particularly if they have difficulty in finding the place.

This applies to both men and women. Readers will see an emphasis throughout on avoiding, or at least reducing, this feeling, as it can mar the opening of a business lunch. You may eat regularly in the restaurant (or in your own premises) and know your way around. Your visitor may not.

Restaurant Staff

Using empathy will make you think differently about restaurant employees. Some people treat restaurant staff as servants in an 'Upstairs Downstairs' manner. Others hardly know they exist as people. I have spoken to business executives who have eaten regularly in the same restaurant (with the same staff) for years, but know absolutely nothing about the employees as people.

Restaurant employees work extremely unsociable hours. It is hot in the kitchen, and hard work serving in a restaurant. They do it because most of them see it as a career, and not just a job. Many consider it a profession. They all like people, otherwise they would never stay in the job.

But many executives treat them as people who blend with the wallpaper. Most of them have families, with children. Sometimes their children take 'O' levels and 'A' levels, or go to university. Waiters do go on holiday! Later in this book you will see the advantage of getting to know the waiters (they will not become over-familiar if they are professionals) and telling them a little about yourself. When you are entertaining they can become your right arm in a sales situation. They can become part of your sales force.

Because of the emphasis on pre-planning and empathy, a large part of the next two chapters deals with a series of points *before* you actually start the meal.

3

Choosing a Restaurant – Stroke your Buyer's Ego

This chapter sets out a series of points to use in deciding where to entertain. It acts as a kind of checklist on whether you might reconsider if the present restaurants you use are as suitable as they should be for successfully entertaining a buyer.

Many of the points are not relevant to entertaining on a social basis. As an example, often people experiment with a new restaurant when they eat out socially. Some people deliberately try somewhere different every time they eat out.

In business entertaining, to create goodwill and to sell, you will see this is not recommended. There is a difference in the two situations. One of the major faults diagnosed on the research for this book is that many executives treat both situations in exactly the same manner.

The points made in the following checklist apply to entertaining in restaurants and cover the middle price to more expensive restaurants, rather than the cheaper restaurants. There may be circumstances where an executive does decide to take out a prospective customer to a cheaper restaurant (possibly if there is a shortage of time), but this book is not written primarily for that set of circumstances.

There are also many executives who feel that the best way to entertain is to take someone to a local pub for lunch. A pub is ideal if you are in a hurry, or where you are entertaining the same person every day for a period. If the pub has character this could be the best place to entertain a foreign buyer. Many pubs have superb buffets or a better style of restaurant than the typical pub lunch.

When you are entertaining on business you must get your client or customer to relax, and a pub may be the most suitable place for this. Should you prefer entertaining in a pub, then many of the key aspects in the checklist would also be applicable.

I do not recommend that you always entertain in the most expensive restaurant in town. Choosing the most expensive place can sometimes rebound when you are selling. What you really have to do is entertain so that you 'stroke your buyer's ego'. This can happen by a whole series of points and not necessarily because the restaurant is very expensive. The situation will vary depending on whether you are entertaining in your territory or whether you are away from your home town in the prospective buyer's territory. In many cases, you will both come from the same large town but possibly from different parts of the town.

Naturally, where you entertain may depend on the size of your budget for entertaining. If your budget is limited then it is better to entertain, say, six times properly, than stretching the budget to entertain ten times.

Some people consider that eating out is expensive. I don't believe it is on business, and this comment is not made because 'the company is paying'.

You know how expensive your own factory, or offices are in rent, rates, and heating. Have you considered you are also paying for these costs in the price of a business meal, often when the restaurant is on a prime site? You can often be more successful by moving out of the office environment to a restaurant, or hotel. It is much more conducive to a sales situation if you choose the right venue. If you spend £30 to £60 for two people on entertaining a client, you are renting between 30 and 40 square feet of valuable space, as well as having an enjoyable meal.

The cost of the meal is relatively low compared with the value of most deals on which executives tend to negotiate. Entertaining customers, or prospective customers in a restaurant is a very cost effective investment – provided you do it right.

1.   Choose two or three restaurants to use regularly as part of your whole sales campaign, so that you create goodwill. The restaurants may be deliberately chosen for various reasons. One may be suitable for an older man, another may be suitable for a younger executive, yet another may be better for foreign visitors if it has a National theme or an internationally known name.

2.   Entertain where you have been before *and* at the same meal period and part of the week. It is a mistake to assume that because you have entertained regularly in a particular restaurant at lunch time, that the same waiter or staff will necessarily be on duty in the evening. In fact, even the menu may be different. Very often the lighting is more subdued. So avoid eating in a restaurant in the evening unless you have entertained there previously.

3.   The same point applies to eating at a different time of the week. Very often the atmosphere, menu and some of the staff may be totally different. As an example, your decision may be to entertain regularly midweek in a particular restaurant because there are other business executives there and everybody is relaxed in the same sort of environment. Should you decide to entertain someone (probably from out of town) at Saturday lunch time, you could find that the restaurant is full of shoppers or families which proves an inappropriate atmosphere for a business lunch.

4.   Research restaurants with your own colleagues carefully before you do any business entertaining in them. Executives experience a threshold barrier in going into a restaurant for the first time. Never entertain in a restaurant where you have not entertained before, unless you are out of town or in special circumstances.

5.   You may have just been moved to an area or just starting to entertain and may not know where to start researching, and which restaurants to try out. If so, ask your colleagues or other local businessmen.

6.   There are many excellent restaurant guide books. I would *not* use them for choosing your specific restaurant before trying them

out first. Ownership of restaurants changes regularly, good chefs often move from job to job. It takes time to inspect premises, assess results, wait for the printer – and then publish the guides. Some of the assessments may be out of date by the time the guide is published.

You cannot risk taking someone out for the first time to a restaurant rated highly by a guide, on an assessment which could be over a year old if you bought the guide late in the year of publication. But you can use restaurant guides in order to pick the targets to research first; so that you end up with the two or three you want to use regularly.

7.   In a large city like London you might have a few regular restaurants on your list, one near your office and another on the other side of town, which could be nearer your prospective buyer's office. Do not choose restaurants which are all convenient for you, rather than your customers.

8.   Apart from the situation where you are entertaining out of town, never risk entertaining in a strange restaurant, even if you are bored. Unless restaurants change their menu regularly it can be repetitive. Many business executives suffer from 'menu fatigue' i.e. they know what is on the menu before they have read it. Even so, do not fall into the temptation of trying somewhere new unless you have researched it very carefully yourself beforehand, at least twice.

9.   Choose a restaurant with a choice of dishes not only to avoid your own menu fatigue but to provide your visitor with more choice. Some restaurants with limited menus can be suitable, if they vary the menu regularly. Often the best food is where there is a limited number of dishes.

There is a trend in many restaurants towards a fixed price menu and the old terms, table d'hote and à la carte are not often printed on menus nowadays. These French terms are used even where the menu does not contain any French dishes, e.g. you could have an à la carte menu in a Chinese restaurant. Many of the finest restaurants have fixed price menus nowadays.

The fixed price menu is a set meal made up of dishes from the à la carte which prices dishes separately. Many restaurants include half a bottle of wine per person in these menus. If you have a limited budget, then fixed price menus can help you stay within your budget without lowering standards.

10.   There may be a situation where you eat with a client or buyer regularly. There are some occasions when you are selling, where there are advantages in letting the prospective customer entertain you particularly when you are in his town. But do not fall into the trap of making this a habit because he is hospitable and always asks you first. Should you have a relationship where you tend to entertain each other alternately, there is no harm is saying 'Why don't we try out a new restaurant and you can (jokingly) blame me if it is awful'. That way you can experiment.

11.   If you are entertaining in a large city, choose the venue which is most suitable, from a transport point of view, for your prospective client, rather than one near your own office or convenient for yourself. One common mistake is to entertain him in a superb restaurant near your own office when he is arriving with a limited time schedule at an airport or station and your office is not near the airport or station.

12.   Choose the restaurant where you feel your prospective buyer will feel most at ease. Choose one which is most suited to the personality, age of your guest, and position in his own organisation, rather than *your* own age or position. It is a mistake to entertain a prospective buyer who is much younger in a restaurant which overawes him, or where the average age of the customer is much higher than that of the young executive. Conversely, I have known young executives entertain an older executive in trendy restaurants which are unsuitable, even if they may be expensive.

13.   Similarly, watch the age of the staff in a restaurant to see that they do not clash with your prospective buyer. Some restaurants have staff who are all young, or all over a certain age bracket. I was due to entertain the chief executive of a leading company and

broke one of my rules by trying a different restaurant. He was older than me, about the same age as the head waiter and many of the waiters. The staff seemed to have a greater affinity with him. They assumed he was paying and I felt very uncomfortable, even more so when they presented him with the bill.

14.   When you are entertaining out of town, many of the points in this checklist are relevant but you will not generally have time to research the particular restaurants. In this case, there is nothing wrong in asking your client where he would like to eat but give him an indication of whether you are on a restricted budget or not.

Say something like, 'I think we both deserve a nice meal tonight' with the emphasis on the word 'nice'. This should tell him, if he has any empathy or understanding at all, that you are not on a tight budget. If you are, you could say 'I hear that the XYZ restaurant is value for money', or a phrase like 'Is there somewhere we could have a quick meal'?

15.   If you are not sure, choose one of the restaurants in the hotel where you are staying. There are many advantages in using the hotel restaurant. Firstly, you can examine the menus beforehand to see if they are suitable. You can check out the menu prices in advance so there are no awkward surprises when you receive the bill. You will also have an opportunity to go into the restaurant before you meet your visitor and introduce yourself (as outlined in the next chapter). Transportation isn't a problem either and you don't have to worry about bad weather. Finally, your visitor probably knows the hotel.

16.   When you are away from your regular restaurant, check that they take your credit cards before you reserve a table.

17.   Some executives consider the customer should be asked to choose the venue. When you are entertaining in *your* own town, never ask the prospective customer to suggest a restaurant unless there are very special circumstances. It may seem a nice gesture to do so. But he has no idea what your budget is, and he may be

worried about recommending the right sort of restaurant and whether this would make a good or bad impact on you. Some people bluff about eating out. He may have given you the impression that he eats in restaurants a lot, but this may be entirely wrong and could embarass him. Never risk this.

You have to control the sales situation as much as possible and if you let your customer choose a restaurant you may well lose the advantages of the situation set out later in this book. If you do wish to ask your client then suggest he chooses from two restaurants you know well, and where they know you well.

18.   Some restaurants have a reception area, or bar area, where you can meet to have an aperitif before going into the restaurant. I remember reading somewhere the phrase that an aperitif is 'a liquid dinner gong' – it alerts the senses for the feast ahead. I like this description.

It is an advantage using a restaurant with an area where you can get your visitor to relax and chat over a drink before you eat. With customers you have entertained before and know well, you may conduct your business first in this area – and then turn the meal into a straightforward social situation.

19.   Some restaurants have a high degree of showmanship. The maître d'hôtel or restaurant manager has a high profile and the restaurant employees are all personalities. This sometimes coincides with a flamboyant style of presentation, with flambéed dishes cooked at the table side.

There is nothing wrong in entertaining in this style of restaurant on a social occasion. Entertaining in this style of restaurant on business would depend on the person(s) being entertained. But be careful if the meal has more of a sales objective than a general goodwill objective. The customer must enjoy the meal experience but he must not be distracted from *your* personality, or your message.

There is a marvellously funny book called Real Men Don't Eat Quiche published by New English Library, which sets out to show in a very tongue in cheek manner, that there are too many quiche eaters around nowadays and not enough real men. The book is about life styles and not just food. But there is a lovely paragraph:

Under no circumstances will a Real Man put up with anything being flambéed at the table. For a start he believes that all the cooking should be done in the kitchen, and secondly it is quite impossible to concentrate on the true purpose of the meal (business, seduction, or keeping the wife happy for the next three months) while some sort of raging inferno is getting out of control two feet away and he knows that at any moment he will be called upon to put out a blazing Italian waiter.

In a sense I am making the same point about entertaining at a 'flamboyant' restaurant when you are selling.

20. There are many restaurants throughout the country which are essentially steak restaurants, or where some of the main dishes on the menu are different types of steak. Steak is very popular and I would not exclude it from your list of restaurants to use, just because the choice is sometimes limited. Much depends on the decor and ambiance of the restaurant – does it stroke your customer's ego? In some cases entertaining in restaurants with a full à la carte menu may oveawe your visitor. You will have to assess his personality and whether he would really enjoy a good steak. Steak restaurants are often good value for money. But never go to them – or any restaurant – because they might be cheaper.

21. Many restaurants have excellent buffet style meals, particularly at lunchtime. Most have cold and hot dishes. There has been a rapid growth in the number of carvery and buffet style restaurants and they have the all important 'visual appeal'.

The one thing they all have in common is a degree of self service, or self-help. Sometimes you have to help yourself to every course. Other times you help yourself to the main course and are served the starter and dessert at the table.

There is nothing wrong in entertaining in this type of restaurant. However, if you are planning to be very specific in your sales approach on that particular occasion, reconsider whether another style restaurant might be better. Should you wish to stress a series of sales points and the many advantages of your services, the whole flow of your sales approach may be interrupted and disjointed by having to get up periodically to collect food. If you have a lot of points to make and ground to cover, interruptions where you both have to leave the table can ruin a sales approach, even from an expert salesman. On the other hand, if you are creating goodwill or have a short presentation to make, there is nothing wrong with self-help carveries and buffet meals as there would be adequate time.

Where you are short of time for the meal or your client has to hurry away, this style of restaurant has the advantage in that you can often reduce the duration of a business lunch by 30 minutes without missing a course.

*   *   *   *   *

These 21 points should enable you to rethink the present restaurants you use or head you in the right direction when you start business entertaining. The main point is not to settle into a rut which suits you but to vary your tactics depending on the circumstances. Whatever you do, try to stroke your guest's ego just a little every time you entertain him.

Gentlemen's Clubs

Some readers will belong to a club, often referred to as a gentlemen's club. These clubs have a history and an image which is unique. It is difficult to become a member and only a small proportion of the total population belong to them. A wealthy person cannot automatically expect to become a member. Should you be a member, I would most certainly use the club for business entertaining in the right circumstances.

One member of a famous club reacted with horror to this suggestion. He said he would resign if too many members began to use the premises for wining and dining businessmen. He stressed very strongly that his club was there primarily for the use of members, their friends and certain V.I.P. visitors.

I would consider a client, or a potential client, to be a V.I.P.

Of course, I realise that if a member began to invite groups of visitors to eat every day, the whole atmosphere of the club would change, and this would be wrong. But I can see no reason why discreet entertaining on a one to one basis should make a serious impact on the character or style of a private club.

Should you belong to a private club I would seriously consider using its facilities for entertaining in a sales situation and where you want to create goodwill. I do not belong to a club and therefore am not sure if I am in a position to be objective about this. But it does make an impression on a visitor.

Sometimes the food is excellent, other times not. But the sense of history is incomparable. There is no doubt that a visitor is going to tell his wife about it and it will stay in the visitor's memory for a long time. I have been entertained at Brookes, The Reform and The Carlton. They were all fascinating experiences and I will not forget the people who invited me.

Should you decide to entertain on business in your club, many of the key points in the next chapter are equally applicable to a club *and* a restaurant.

Don't forget that the club will have a fascinating history which you know about but your visitor may not. It is worthwhile explaining it's origins and history. Some of the paintings and portraits are valuable. Do not assume that a visitor recognises all the well known people in the portraits.

In the last James Bond film with Sean Connery, Never Say Never Again, Bond's boss, M, outlines near the beginning of the film, the most dangerous assignment imaginable to 007 – so dangerous Bond could hardly survive.

Bond gulps and asks what will be his reward if he is successful and survives. His boss M looks at him and says: 'A very special reward . . . I will take you out to dine at my club.'

Provided the visitor is not patronised, I have no doubt that entertaining at a gentlemen's club can be very impressive, and an invaluable aid to improving goodwill, increasing sales, or clinching a major contract.

4

Executive Entertaining in a Restaurant

The previous chapter deals with choosing the right restaurants – and whether to use your club. The following checklist points cover the actual situation after you have chosen a venue and have become known as a regular. Where you are just starting to entertain, these points will assist you to become a regular.

Some of the points are obvious but worth re-emphasising. Generally they cover the situation where you are entertaining someone for the first time or you have entertained them before but in a different restaurant. This is a much more sensitive situation than entertaining a client or customer in the same restaurant for the second or third time.

You may find that your client has eaten in the restaurant before and, of course, you will find this out when you fix a time and a place. The first series of points in the checklist assume that he has not been to the restaurant before.

In discussing this book with various executives, many asked who would a restaurant consider to be a good or regular customer? Many executives feel you have to eat in a restaurant at least once a week in order to be considered as a regular and treated as a good customer.

Many restaurants have customers who eat once a week, or more often. But this is generally a small proportion. If you entertain in a restaurant once a month you would be considered by many restaurant owners as a very good customer. Many restaurateurs would like to have *more* customers who entertain once a month.

But if you have an account and follow the basic human relations points set out in this chapter, even if you only eat once every three months the restaurant staff will recognise you and treat you as a very worthwhile customer.

1. Define and set your objectives for the lunch very clearly beforehand. If necessary, write them down. It could be that the luncheon is not part of a longer period of selling but the only opportunity you have to sell. It is therefore, even more important to set yourself objectives. Many executives make a basic mistake in expecting to get an order or to clinch a deal in every sales situation. Often this is not likely over a luncheon, unless the deal is very advanced and the luncheon is really an opportunity to finalise a few points and agree a sale.

The objective may be just to move the sales situation forward; it is in any case a great opportunity to get to know the buyer and his company. It should give you valuable clues on whether he is a decision maker or an adviser to the decision maker. It will be very clear whether the luncheon is of a celebratory nature because the deal has been clinched, and an opportunity to thank your buyer or client and create goodwill. Whatever the objective, most of the following points are relevant.

It is critically important to perceive that your client (customer) is relaxed, enjoying the meal, and is receptive to any sales message you wish to put across. Some people feel ill at ease in a restaurant, particularly the first time they are there. It is important that you see your guest is comfortable and at ease. He is a strange person or strange 'animal' going into a strange cave for the first time. No one has researched why people feel ill at ease in a new restaurant when they do not feel this way in other premises.

Face to face selling has many advantages over other kinds of selling, e.g. telephone selling or sales letters. One of them is that it is the only sales situation where you can practice non-verbal communication and body language.

The first-time visitor to a restaurant will often spend time looking around. This is the wrong time to make any kind of sales point. You will often see that in a strange restaurant many people do not sit upon the whole chair. When they first sit down – they sit on the front two thirds and they do not lean back. But at a certain point, they will shift their weight and lean back, i.e. they begin to relax.

This will usually happen at one of two points. Firstly, when they have ordered and hand the menu back to the waiter, or, secondly, when they have finished their first course. If they are still sitting forward on the front of their chair by then, it is an indication that there is something wrong with the restaurant, or your handling of the situation. These non-verbal situations show you the point when your guest is more likely to be receptive to what you are saying.

2.   If the business entertaining takes place at lunch or in the evening and is part of a continuous sales situation, *never* delegate the entertaining to a younger executive. Sometimes, there is a tendency with chief executives who are extremely busy, to work together with a team and the prospective buyer, but then to leave the entertaining to other executives. This is always wrong. If it is worthwhile spending your time selling all morning, then it is worthwhile 'stroking the client's ego' by spending lunch time with him.

This was one of the errors in the situation described in the first chapter.

3.   If the luncheon is not part of the total sales situation and you are just meeting the customer for a meal, find out how he is going to get to the restaurant. If he is staying at a hotel in town, you could pick him up by car or divert your taxi to meet him before you go on to the restaurant. Where he is arriving by car, try to make sure that there are parking facilities available, or tell him where he can park.

4.   Some entrances to restaurants are confusing, particularly some hotel restaurants. Make sure the customer knows the location of

the restaurant quite clearly. It is not sufficient to just say 'I will meet you at the XYZ restaurant'. There are a number of restaurants within hotels where the entrance to the hotel is not too clear.

As examples, The Savoy Hotel is on the Embankment, and the Park Lane Hotel is in Park Lane. But a first time visitor should be told that the main entrance to the Savoy is in the Strand, and the entrance to the Park Lane Hotel is in Brick Street.

There are some other well known restaurants in London which are very difficult to find for a first-time visitor. Try to find the highly successful Joe Allens in Exeter Street or the Greenhouse in Hays Mews, without directions. I know one five star hotel, the Piccadilly in Manchester with extremely good restaurants, where it is virtually impossible to find the way in if you are driving or walking for the first time, unless you ask.

5.   Many hotels have more than one restaurant and it is important to remember that the prospective buyer may not know this. This is particularly relevant if the restaurants have a name. I well remember making this mistake myself in saying to a client 'Meet me at the XYZ hotel in the bar which is adjacent to the restaurant', without specifying the name of the restaurant. I thought he was late but he was actually sitting in the bar adjacent to the other restaurant which had another name. A restaurant complex may have different restaurants, for example The Swiss Centre, on different floors.

6.   Many of these points may seem obvious but they are worth repeating because there is nothing worse than waiting in a strange place on your own for the first time. Be specific about where you are going to meet – in the hotel lobby or in the bar, and specify which bar. Some restaurants have a very small waiting area or bar area, which fills up quickly. If this is the case, specify 'You will meet in the bar area, or if this is full, at a table'.

7.   Make sure that you are there first. Whatever you do, plan to be there at least fifteen minutes before the agreed time. There are many reasons why people are late. In selling there are absolutely

no excuses for being late. If the traffic is bad then it is your fault for not allowing for this possibility. It is far better for you to wait than to keep the customer waiting.

People who are habitually late often cannot delegate, and certainly should not be in selling. Some years ago I attended a course on selling which started at 9.00 a.m. At 9.01 a.m. the doors were shut to make a point to latecomers, even though they were paying a high fee.

8.   Of course there can be exceptional circumstances when you are going to be late. I was once stopped 50 yards from the entrance to a hotel by the police because there was a bomb scare, and there was no way I could get into the hotel. If you are going to be late, telephone the restaurant yourself, or, get someone else to telephone for you.

Speak to the head waiter or restaurant manager and make sure that they know the name of the guest and that they offer him a drink, apologising for the fact that you are going to be late. This can help to smooth over a difficult start to a sales situation.

9.   If you want to be recognised by the staff and you are just starting to use a restaurant, go in at a quieter period (before 12.30 p.m.) introduce yourself to the owner or head waiter and tell him you are planning to use his restaurant regularly.

10.   Give them your name in the restaurant. Don't wait for them to learn it. Give them your visiting card and if you consider it desirable, tell them who you are and what you do.

Very few people do this but with empathy you realise that many restaurant staff can be bored by the sheer repetitiveness of the job. On the other hand, they are really only in that business if they like people. They may talk to other staff or go home and say something like 'You know that Mr Smith I told you about, who comes in once a month, I found out today that he is an engineer'.

Nowadays, if you are heading a major organisation it might be advisable, for security reasons, not to let them know who you are and what you do, although if you are well known most good restaurants will find out who you are. Restaurant staff are going to remember your name and use it in front of your prospective buyer if they know a little about you.

11.   In time, find out about the restaurant staff. Do not treat them as people who 'blend with the wallpaper'. Find out a little about their families. Ask them about *their* holiday.

12.   Make sure that your name is also used by cloakroom staff and toilet attendants, if the restaurant employs them. I entertain regularly in one restaurant where the toilet attendant, Michael, chats whenever we meet. This seems to impress the people I am entertaining, in some cases more so than if the restaurant manager recognises me.

13.   If you think it appropriate, tell the restaurant manager the name of your guest. When you are well known in the restaurant it is a nice gesture to introduce your client to the restaurant manager and your waiter, and then make sure that they use *his* name. In fact, it is preferential in this situation that they use his name more often than yours. You can encourage them to do this by using his name in their presence, 'Mr Greene will have melon'.

14.   Try to get a specific table whenever you entertain. This is not always possible unless you entertain in a restaurant regularly, but there are some tables where you will be disturbed less and where it is easier to sell than others. It is well worthwhile researching these and trying to obtain that table. Make a note in your diary of the actual table number(s) and when you reserve a table next time ask for it.

However far in advance you reserve a table and however regular you entertain in a restaurant, there will be times when you cannot be given a special table. Be tolerant if this happens on occasions. It is quite a skill in planning the seating arrangements for a busy restaurant. Sometimes head waiters need the judgement of Solomon when two, or more, regular guests all ask for the same table at the same time.

15.   Don't forget to reserve a table, or make sure your secretary does. Some executives don't bother. I have seen the same executives who eat regularly in a restaurant without booking, become very angry when they stroll in with a client during the Christmas period, or a busy day, and find they cannot get a table.

16.   I tend to book a table myself because it gives me an opportunity to chat and put across a message if it is a particularly important luncheon, and to make sure I get a good table. This is a key point in getting the restaurant staff as part of your sales team (see point 30).

17.   If you have a 'common' name like Smith, Greene, or Green, it is easy for the staff to have a mix-up. So make sure they get your initials as well when you book. I even mention my first name as well to avoid any possible confusion.

18.   In establishing a relationship with restaurant staff, put yourself in their shoes. If it is practical telephone them if you are going to be late. Earlier I mentioned that *you* should not be late when your client is going there direct. Sometimes your client will telephone to say he will be late. Or you are working with him on a particularly important point and decide to finalise it before going to lunch.

When you are going to be more than 15 minutes late, telephone the restaurant to say so. Otherwise they may keep a reservation for you but give the better table to someone else.

19.   When you cancel lunch always contact the restaurant as soon as you know, so that they have a chance to re-sell the table. When you are selling this may occur when your client cancels, or sometimes when you just do not have sufficient time. Some executives believe a restaurant can always re-sell the table, so they don't bother to telephone. Other executives think that restaurants are so profitable that it doesn't matter if they do not turn up. Nothing could be more incorrect.

Restaurants have two major costs: food and drink, and payroll, both of which can range from 55 to 75 per cent. Added to this are menu costs, laundry, replacement of cutlery and crockery, heat, light, and cooking costs, depreciation of furniture and kitchen equipment. All pay rates and water rates. Many pay high rents.

So you will often find the Net Profit of a restaurant is no more than 10 per cent of sales. In a 60-seat restaurant, a loss of four or six customers through bookings that do not materialise, could mean no profit at all for that meal period. If you really want the restaurateur to help you when you are selling, help him by telephoning if you are going to be more than fifteen minutes late, or immediately you know you have to cancel.

20.   As the meal progresses, you should ensure that the customer becomes more and more attentive to your sales approach, so that nothing deflects from the objectives set before the start of the luncheon – even going to the toilet can totally ruin a sales approach during a meal. There is nothing quite as bad mannered as leaving your customer sitting at the table, it can destroy a natural steady progression of the sales approach.

21.   Most restaurants tend to have a kind of thoroughfare where there is more activity with waiters and wine waiters moving around. Some positions for a table look good, but in practice can be right in the middle of a busy route.

On your research and visits to the restaurant, watch carefully to see where there is most activity by staff. This generally is in the line leading from the kitchen to the cashier, or to and from the bar. In some restaurants the cashier is located by the kitchens which means the place to avoid is a table near the 'in' and 'out' doors. Other restaurants have a cashier near the exit so there are two busy thoroughfares. Sometimes the wine dispense point is located in a third position which creates three thoroughfares.

22.   Some restaurants have a side which is considered to be the V.I.P. side. In practice, this should be the one with the best view, either out of the window or of the whole restaurant. But quite often I find there is no reason to the V.I.P. side. This has probably just developed for some 'historical' reason which no one can

remember. Try to find out what is the V.I.P. side when you first begin to use the restaurant. If it isn't obvious, ask the staff when you are on your own.

23.   Other restaurants do have a good side and naturally if there is a particularly nice view (for example, overlooking a park) this is the side on which to try to obtain a seat.

I have never believed it is worthwhile bribing (tipping heavily) to obtain a good table, although this practice is quite common in America. I have worked in America, and visited regularly. I never resorted to the heavy tipping that some people do (when they are shown to a table). But I did build a relationship when I could with the restaurant staff so that in time I received good service without having to tip more than the norm. If you have taken the previous advice of getting to know the staff (not just the head waiter) there is a strong likelihood that you will be seated at one of the best tables.

24.   Always seat your guest with his face to the view, or if there is no view, with his back to the wall looking out over the restaurant. No one has quite analysed the sociological reason why people prefer to sit with their back to the wall. Some people say it dates back thousands of years to the caveman instinct. People feel more safe, more secure that way.

You will be well known to the restaurant's staff as a worthwhile customer and consequently I have often seen the person paying, namely yourself, to be seated with his back to the wall, i.e. in the best seat. This is wrong. It is important that the client is given preferential treatment, even if it means that you have no view whatsoever. Where restaurants have low partitions in the centre, then the next best alternative is for your client to sit with his back against the partition. Whatever happens, try to avoid being in the middle of a large restaurant.

25.   Before you go in, think how you want to seat people if there are more than two. When there are four or more, seat the most important decision maker in the best position, with the view or his

back to the wall. When it is a two to two situation you will not necessarily sit alternately. In some sales situations, your guests may wish to sit next to each other so that they can communicate more easily. In some selling/buying situations they may decide that one of them will ask all the questions and do all the talking. This could mean that the other person may wish to pass a note to his colleague.

I remember a situation when I was negotiating with my client for the sale of a hotel to a very wealthy and well known hotelier. Like many wealthy people he disliked having to deal direct and had one of his executives do all the talking.

They asked to sit next to each other. I named a price over coffee. At this point the millionaire wrote a note on a small piece of paper and gave it to his executive who went very quiet. I, in turn, didn't know what to do and assumed they weren't too interested. My client, the owner of the hotel, promptly stepped in and reduced the price which was immediately accepted by the buyer. They shook hands on the deal.

As we left I went back to the table to put a cash tip in with the signed bill and saw the screwed up message in the ashtray. I just had to read it. It said, 'Say nothing'.

26.   Where the meal is just to create goodwill, or to celebrate a sale, or a deal, it is usually better to seat the four people alternately.

27.   Where you have more than four people, always warn the restaurant well beforehand so that they may find the best position for a larger table.

28.   Where you have more than four, consider whether it might be more conducive to a sales situation if you booked a small private room. Many restaurants have them and virtually every hotel has a number of private dining rooms to take around six people or more. Many banqueting premises are ideal for the smaller private meal, and specialise in this activity. Alternatively, some restaurants do not have a private room but have an alcove, or area which is more suited for a private type of meal.

29.   Where there are three people at a table for four, always make sure the restaurant staff take away the cutlery and crockery for the fourth place. Most good restaurants will do this automatically but some may forget if they are busy.

30.   It is important that the main meal should go perfectly and you should have coffee, brandies and cigars at the right time. If you are going to make a specific sales pitch at a certain point, there is absolutely no reason why you should not telephone the restaurant manager beforehand and tell him about it. In fact, on a number of occasions I have deliberately gone into the restaurant beforehand, rather than telephoning, in order to tell the head waiter that the lunch is of vital importance.

On a particular occasion, I had virtually agreed the sale of a hotel by one hotelier to another, except that we had a key point to settle on the split of the total purchase price between property, and furniture, fixtures and equipment.

I went into the restaurant and told the head waiter that as soon as his staff had poured the coffee and checked whether anyone wanted brandies, he was then to leave us for 15 minutes before he asked whether anyone wanted even a refill of coffee. You can cover a lot of ground in 15 minutes. Both my client and the purchaser realised that this was the important time to settle something without being interrupted by a waiter.

31.   Before you entertain someone for the first time, you should find out whether your client has any special preferences or any food he does not eat. He may be a Muslim, Jew, vegetarian or vegan, or may be allergic to some foods. One advantage of going to a restaurant with a more extensive menu is that you can generally find something which suits all palates and tastes.

You can ask the person direct, or you can get your secretary to check with his secretary about his preferences, or any special diet. People on a special diet, e.g. a diabetic, are no longer inhibited about saying so.

This is one occasion where I think it is possible to say to someone, 'Perhaps the ABC will not have your kind of food and you may care to suggest one'. This may arise when you are entertaining a Muslim or a Jew. Be careful how this is handled because most Jewish people will eat anything nowadays and many British Muslims also have a wide palate.

I have found when I am entertaining Muslims from abroad, they will usually give me an indication when we talk about having lunch, of their eating preferences and whether they drink. It is important to remember that there are large Muslim communities that do not come from the Arab countries, for example, the Hausers, with about 50 million people in Northern Nigeria. Most people think of Arabs as Muslims. There are many Christian Arabs, and a large British Muslim community, formally from Pakistan or East Africa. All tend to have different diets.

32.   There are many French restaurants in Britain where, naturally, the menu is in French. There are a large number of other restaurants where the menu is written in French, although the dishes are not necessarily French. It is not within the scope of this book to debate whether or not it is a good thing to have menus written in French in this country. Many hotel restaurants tend to have the menu written in French and I often entertain in restaurants where this is the case. No doubt there are times when you have done so.

Some restaurateurs write their menus in French because they believe they can charge more by doing so. There are many kinds of French cooking. There is classical, based on the recipes in the Guide Culinaire. There is regional which I feel is more like the food in France – outside the large cities. There is bistro, and there is cuisine moderne, or modern French cooking.

Find out whether the owner, or the chef have worked in France or French-speaking Switzerland. They do not have to be French, because there are many British restaurateurs and chefs who produce superb French food. If they have worked in France – even for a relatively short time – that is a place to eat – for French food.

33.   Even if your knowledge of French menus is extremely good your client may not speak a word of French, and he may not tell

you this. It is important never to make your customer feel ill at ease, or to lose face. If you are going to entertain in a restaurant where the menu is in French, make sure it is a menu which has English translations as well. If this is not the case, always ask the head waiter to translate even if *you* understand every particular dish. This should overcome the problem of your customer feeling slightly inferior because you appear to understand the menu and he does not.

I entertain regularly in one well known restaurant which has a menu in French. I think they had a considerable battle with the executive chef who is French, and they ended up with a compromise. The à la carte menu is in French with no translations but the fixed price menu has the main courses translated in English and the starters and desserts in French.

Quite often when I am entertaining in this restaurant, I find that my guest will choose the main course *first* because it is in English, but he will pause and hesitate over the starter. At that point the waiter is not always around to take the order and to translate, so I generally suggest two or three starters in English which I feel are very good, for example, 'the whitebait is particularly good here'.

Should you find that you entertain in a restaurant with a French menu and your French is not good, state this right at the beginning – your guest may know more than you. Say something like, 'I eat here regularly because the food is so good but the menu often confuses me'.

34.   You will have to make a decision whether you eat dishes cooked in garlic and highly seasoned food depending on what you are going to do after the meal. If you have meetings with people who haven't had a similar dish with you, you should consider avoiding dishes cooked in garlic and strong spices.

35.   Many people entertain in what are now called ethnic restaurants (Greek, Chinese, Indian). Exactly the same principles apply in getting to know the restaurant and the staff getting to know you.

In the case of ethnic restaurants, it is even more important to ask whether people like that kind of cooking before you book a table. There are many people who are very adventurous in their eating but do not like, say, a curry. It is a mistake to assume that everyone is adventurous in their eating habits. I used to entertain regularly in a Greek restaurant and found that many people liked eating there for a change. But every so often I sensed that they were rather unsure about Greek food and, if this was the case, I always took them somewhere else.

36.   There are some restaurants that have a number of menus without prices, which are handed to the guest. The idea behind this is a kind of politeness in that the guest should not have to worry about prices, as the host is paying for the meal. I find that this tends to confuse people. Even if they are not paying for the meal, many people in a buying situation do not wish to appear greedy and have the most expensive items on the menu, or, alternatively look cheap and order the lower priced items. Without prices they could be at a loss what to choose.

If you are selling I see no reason why a guest should not receive a menu with prices, and cannot understand the advantage of handing him a menu without prices.

37.   Often restaurants will have a fixed price menu *and* an à la carte menu. Wherever there is both, always say to your customer 'please choose from the à la carte if you want to'.

38.   Always ascertain beforehand whether your customer is limited in the amount of time he has available – what I call a time sensitive situation. This applies to many businessmen at lunch time.

There are some restaurants where it is virtually impossible to have a meal in under 1½ hours and many businessmen would like to be fed in under one hour, if they have a meeting to go to. If your guest is time sensitive, always let the restaurant know well in advance and specify that you must be out by a certain time (say, 2.15 p.m.). Repeat this when you order. Do not say 'within an hour' as the head waiter may forget what time you sat down and one hour may become longer. They should write a note on the kitchen check and say something as well when they take your order into the kitchen.

In this situation, make sure that they present the bill to you when you are having coffee. In some restaurants, you can have a good meal in 45 minutes and then have to wait a long time for the bill. If there is any likelihood that delivery of the bill and payment is going to take time, then tell the head waiter you will be back in a moment and leave the table with your guest, returning to settle the bill later.

This time sensitive situation is when you might consider a carvery or buffet style restaurant, for you can dictate your own time rather than that of the kitchen.

39.   In entertaining in a sales situation, you have to avoid looking mean; it is amazing how many people hate spending money. I was once entertained by a man who spent all his time telling me that he thought restaurant prices were far too high!

On the other hand, avoid appearing to be 'splashing money around'. Some buyers believe that, indirectly, they are paying for the lunch anyhow. If it appears that the person selling has an abundance of money, the buyer may consider that he doesn't really need the extra business or that his margins are too high.

40.   During my research with executives, one subject which came up time and time again, was the question of smoking when you are entertaining on business. The statistics show an overwhelming trend towards giving up smoking cigarettes. Not only do the anti smoking campaigns make more smokers conscious of the dangers of smoking, but they have also made non smokers much more aware of the smell of stale tobacco smoke. If you study the non smoking areas on airlines and underground systems in the world, you will see a steady increase in their numbers. Some larger restaurants have non smoking areas. Many hotels have non smoker bedrooms.

More smokers raised this subject with me, than non smokers. The basic problem is should you smoke if you find that your customer or prospective customer does not? I am excluding offering cigars at the end of a meal.

I am a non smoker but I have thought about this very carefully and discussed it at length with smokers and non smokers. What I believe should happen is that a smoker should try to abstain from smoking during the course of the meal. But if he is a heavy smoker and it becomes extremely difficult for him not to smoke at all, then it is silly for him to become tense during the meal by abstaining.

The danger is that he may hurry the meal along in order to get to the point where he can smoke. Before smoking, he should ask first, in case his customer has strong objections, and he should ask before taking out a cigarette. What sometimes happens is that the smoker takes out a cigarette and practically lights it before saying 'Do you mind if I smoke?' If you are really keen to create goodwill, and obtain that contract, then you should refrain from smoking if your potential customer objects.

41.   Ask the customer's preference for wine. People who drink wine a lot generally tend to find that their palate prefers a drier wine as the years go by. On the other hand, a buyer might prefer a sweeter wine or a medium/sweet.

The experts will tell you that you should drink red wine with beef and white wine with fish, but if your potential buyer wants white wine with beef, then that is his preference and he should receive it. There has been a trend away from red wines towards people drinking white wines and there are various reasons for this. One is that some white wines generally have a lower calorie count. Secondly many people prefer to drink a wine which is slightly chilled and therefore choose a white wine. Lastly, white wines are generally lighter. Whatever your customer chooses this is the wine that you should order.

Some wine waiters show, by the expression on their faces, that you have chosen the wrong wine for the specific food you have ordered. This doesn't matter as long as you have ordered what your customer wants.

42.   You may have had a very tough morning. You could have had a row with your wife. It may be that you have nearly clinched the order and feel like relaxing, or you may feel tense. Whatever the circumstances, avoid the temptation to over-drink. You cannot control the whole sales situation if you have had too many drinks before or during the meal and two many brandies afterwards.

On the other hand, if your client is in the mood to drink let him do so, and appear not to be too far behind. If he wants a second brandy, order a second one for yourself but do not necessarily drink all of it.

43.   There appears to be a steadily increasing number of people who do not drink alcohol. In particular, this seems to apply at lunch time rather than in the evening, or when someone is driving. Sometimes the person is teetotal; other times he just has a busy afternoon and deliberately chooses not to have anything to drink at lunch time.

If you find when you are entertaining that the customer does not wish to drink, it could be a mistake if you decide to do the same. He may not wish to impose his non drinking habits on you. Naturally, you should not over-drink but there is no reason why you should not have a glass of wine. Don't stop drinking because he cannot for health reasons. It could be misplaced sympathy. If a customer has a health problem which stops him from drinking, it may well make him feel extremely awkward by suggesting that you do not drink as well.

44. It is the normal practice nowadays to order mineral water with the meal, even if you are both drinking wine. I believe it is a good touch to do so. It is vital to do so if he, or both of you, are not drinking.

45. One of the dangers of business entertaining is that it is very easy to relax, enjoy yourself, and forget the business objectives. Sometimes, the objective is just to make one key sales point and to make sure that your guest remembers it. Many people begin to enjoy themselves and then remember the key sales point when shaking the customer's hand, or after he has just left.

46. Give him a chance to eat. Often in selling it is important to take the opportunity to do some research and ask the prospective customer a number of questions. These could be about him personally so that you get to know him better, or could be about his company. As you all know asking questions and this kind of research is important. But when you are entertaining him make sure that it does not spoil your customer's meal. On the other hand, if he wants to ask you questions and chat away, it does not matter if your meal is ruined provided he enjoys the food and the atmosphere.

My advice is to talk generally and start any main selling points (if you are going to make them) after the main course. Then be more specific after dessert, unless your earlier questioning has shown that he is short of time.

47. Always ask whether your guest would like liqueurs or brandies, and whether he would like a cigar. There are a number

of executives who will not have a brandy after a meal because they are going back to work, but would like a cigar. Many people who do not smoke cigarettes do smoke cigars. Some women do. Offering a cigar adds a nice touch at the end of a meal.

Under no circumstances suggest that they might like to take a cigar to smoke later. It may surprise readers but more than once I have been entertained by someone who very expansively has ordered a cigar for me, put it in my top pocket and suggested that I might like to smoke it later.

48.   At the point during the meal when you are near to asking for the bill do not ask for it if you still have some key points to make, and have not achieved your objective. Asking for the bill is in a sense 'closing' the whole sales situation and it may be too early. On the other hand, if the lunch is part of a whole sales sequence and you are due to go back to the factory or office, then there is nothing wrong in making sure that the bill is presented promptly.

49.   There are only four ways of settling the bill – by credit card, signing on agreed charge terms, payment by cheque or cash. We are riddled in our society with a whole series of status points, some of which impress people and others which do not. For some reason it is less impressive to pay by actual cash. Credit card companies now have special cards which add status. A number of the larger hotels and restaurant companies have their own 'clubs' with a distinct card. In a sense these cards stroke the holder's ego.

Paying by cheque against a bankers card, or by credit card are quite acceptable. But signing the account adds a tone which is difficult to explain. It arises because you are obviously known in the restaurant and have been there many times before. Most restaurants are only too pleased to open a credit account for you, subject to taking out references, and you do not necessarily need to have eaten there many times in the past.

50.   If you decide to tip in addition to any possible service charge, then I would suggest leaving cash rather than writing the tip on the bill or credit card slip. The whole subject of tipping is so important that this has been covered in Chapter 13.

51.   At this point the luncheon situation is basically over – or is it? If you are returning to your own premises in order to continue the sales situation then it is over. But many people make the mistake of spending a lot of money, time, care and attention on taking someone out to lunch, then they shake hands and leave. This is fine from a social point of view or if you are buying. But if you are selling then your work is not completely over.

52.   If your visitor is parked nearby, make sure he has no problem in getting to the car park and away. It is quite possible that after two or more hours sitting in a restaurant, the first time visitor may have forgotten the exact location of the car park if it is not immediately behind the restaurant. I generally make a point of walking with my guest to the car park in order to make sure that there is no problem and then waving them goodbye.

I do this now because in the past, people have telephoned me to say they couldn't get out of the car park for another 30 minutes because they were blocked in by some 'idiot'. It is possible to lose the whole benefit of a good sales luncheon by not making sure that your guest is away without any problems. One experienced sales executive I know walks to the car park with his customer to see what car he drives.

53.   Similarly, if you are both going to catch a taxi in different directions, make sure that he is given the first one, even if you have to wait around.

54.   If you have a car (or chauffeur) and he does not, then offer to drop him off at some convenient point. I have never known people to take advantage of this. It always makes a good impression on me when people offer to go out of their way to drop me off somewhere. This kind of point is more important than many people imagine. It is not only good selling, but good manners.

55.   There will often be a situation where the luncheon is quite separate to other sales situations where the client, or prospective client, is not with you throughout the day. As in every sales situation, you must set aside a few quiet minutes to ask yourself

whether you achieved the objective(s) you set for yourself at the start of the meal; and if you did not, why not?

56.   Do not forget to follow up the luncheon, if appropriate, with the required information and action leading to the next step and a successful close.

*   *   *   *   *

As well as checking whether you have achieved your objective, I would urge you to spend around 15 minutes going through this chapter again in order to check whether you have gone wrong in the past, why, and how you can improve aspects in the future.

Not all the points in the checklist will be appropriate to your own particular circumstances, but most will. You will often find that the best laid plans go wrong. I have had some disastrous business meals when I rushed things and did not pre-prepare. More often it arose when I broke my own rules and tried somewhere new without spending time on research first.

During my research a number of executives asked me about entertaining and meetings over breakfast. In America, breakfast meetings are very common and this is a developing trend in Europe. There are many more restaurants open for breakfast in America than in Europe where breakfast meetings tend to take place in a hotel dining room or hotel restaurant.

Some people enjoy breakfast meetings and if you do – fine! But I believe they should be thought of as meetings and not sales situations – unless a potential buyer specifically requests them. Many people are 'morning' people, but I suspect many more are not. When you are selling, inviting a prospective customer to breakfast will not make him as receptive to your ideas as inviting him to lunch or dinner. Even if he is staying in the hotel, many people like to have breakfast by themselves, collect their thoughts and read a newspaper before the day's work begins.

Breakfast meetings are fine just for a meeting, when time is very short during the day. But as a sales situation I think they leave a lot to be desired and should be avoided, unless the buyer specifically requests one.

5

Female Executives – Entertaining

Selling is only one aspect of marketing, and markets are changing constantly. There are dozens of definitions of marketing. This is not a book on marketing but about one aspect of face to face selling – namely entertaining customers.

But I cannot resist including one definition of marketing by Anderson and Lembke because it has a slightly different emphasis:—

> We believe that the real meaning of marketing is listening to the demands of the market and satisfying those demands at a profit. From this it follows that superior marketing is listening to the market more intently than your competitors and satisfying the demands more effectively.

Social and sociological changes create new marketing opportunities. One significant social change which creates considerable market opportunities is the move of women into executive positions. Many businessmen (and even some businesswomen) overlook and underestimate the market opportunities this creates.

They are not 'listening to the demands of the market'.

Women have worked for a long time. But it is only recently that women have started to climb the executive ladder. This trend is still in its infancy. Many women executives are in selling. It means that many more women are travelling, staying in hotels and eating out on business.

Very few statistics are available on women executives who travel and are therefore likely to entertain and be entertained. Most available research on women travellers is in America. This shows that the average travelling woman executive is six years younger than her male counterpart. She tends to be in sales, marketing, public and press relations, or personnel work, and makes ten to twelve trips per year, tending to stay away longer than a man. Some 3.7 million businesses in the United States are now owned by women. The majority are in retail and service businesses. Seventy-six per cent founded their own business rather than inherited it from a father or husband. A similar trend is starting in Europe.

So we have a situation where, since the start of this decade, the situation has changed from men generally entertaining men to:—

men entertaining women

women entertaining men

women entertaining women

In discussing this subject with female executives some say the last situation is the most difficult.

As a generalisation, the situation is no different to the main Chapters 3 and 4 in this book. Virtually all of the key checklist points are equally applicable to entertaining when the person selling is a women, or the potential buyer is a women, or both are.

The main difference is that to a certain extent both parties are unused to the situation and on slightly unfamiliar ground. Many very experienced businessmen find it strange to have to sell to a woman and worry about entertaining them.

Some don't do it at all. A senior director confessed to me he always arranged his programme so that he took a male visitor to lunch. Another director said he did the opposite, so he could 'relax completely and not work!'. These attitudes will change when it is realised that more and more women are major decision makers in a buying situation, or advisers to a key decision maker.

Men Entertaining Women

1. The importance of picking the right venue is crucial. There are some restaurants where women feel less at ease even if they eat out regularly on business. There are other restaurants where they feel immediately at ease and, therefore, more receptive to your sales approach.

It is difficult to understand why. It could be the decor, the lighting, the menu, or the staff. Much depends on the opening greeting and welcome by the restaurant staff. In London, I only use two restaurants for entertaining women clients because experience tells me they like them better than any others. And yet they are two totally different style restaurants although the spend on the bill is very nearly the same.

2. Again it comes down to research and learning from mistakes. The best thing is to research different restaurants with your wife, secretary or a female colleague at work. Tell them the reason why you are entertaining them and then ask for a critique after.

3. Don't just ask them about the food, decor and service but about the cloakrooms and toilets as well. Male readers may think I am being pedantic about toilets but female readers will understand. They are very important to many women.

Most hotels and restaurants are designed and built by men for men. In some cases the facilities in the Ladies toilet are totally inadequate. Have you noticed in public places like tourist attractions on a sunny day, there is always a longer queue outside 'the Ladies'? The same situation usually applies to most toilet facilities attached to function rooms and to toilets in restaurants. Most restaurants dealing with a business market have toilet facilities designed on the assumption that there will be virtually an all male custom sitting at the tables.

When you are selling, it is important that nothing disturbs the chemistry of the whole sales situation. Nothing should cause the slightest annoyance. You could say 'So what, I didn't create the lack of toilet facilities'. But you chose the venue and she (the buyer) may get irritated with the restaurant and, indirectly, with you. The only way you are going to find out about this slight problem is to use other women in your research, before settling the decision on which restaurant you will use.

4.   Some good restaurants are in exclusive hotels where the owners deliberately use no signposting. The argument is that a hotel should be like a large attractive private house, and there are no signs in private homes. I remember sitting with my wife, in Cyprus, at a luncheon with some top hoteliers and the conversation was that signs are rather 'vulgar'.

I am not sure I agree. Not too long ago, I was invited to lunch by someone who was going to persuade me that I needed their firm's services. The venue was in an exclusive five star hotel and I had never been there before. I arrived and couldn't find the toilet, because there were no signs. Eventually, I walked into the Ladies by mistake. Embarrassed, I asked an assistant manager why they had no signs on the toilets. He told me 'They are not necessary, all our regular guests *know* where they are . . . sir!' This made me feel four feet tall. What about the guests of the regular guests? This situation could be more awkward for your customer if she is a woman.

I see no reason why hotels and restaurants cannot have discreet signs which are not vulgar. But if you choose a venue with no signs make sure that you direct her (or him) to the bar or lounge where you are meeting, or you ask them to check with reception or the concierge when they arrive 'because it is difficult to locate the first time'.

5.   There are some women (usually a minority) who enjoy going to a restaurant where the customers are exclusively male. If you are in a delicate stage of selling this could be inadvisable. Choose a restaurant where there are a high proportion – not necessarily a majority – of women eating. This shows that women like the place.

6.   The reverse also applies. I remember entertaining a client in a

restaurant in Knightsbridge which was nearly full of women shoppers. Somehow we hardly spoke about business. I didn't achieve my objectives and had to have another meeting with him. It was a pleasant lunch but the environment was all wrong for a business luncheon.

7.   Avoid the temptation to show off. We have all seen *other* executives entertaining women on business who go over the top by showing off their gourmet knowledge of food, their experience of the best wines, and by tipping ostentatiously.

This may work if the objective is to impress a young inexperienced businesswoman. But at that age she probably is not even an adviser to the decision maker. A more experienced woman may smile and be friendly, but may place future orders for your products with your competitors.

8.   Many men ask 'What do you talk about? You can't talk shop the whole time and you can hardly ask whether she saw the winning goal in the European Cup Final on the television last night'. The answer is that you don't necessarily have to talk much except when you make key points on the advantages of your services or products, or if you try to close.

You ask questions. She talks. You listen. I once had lunch with a woman T.V. producer because I thought – wrongly – that I could obtain some free publicity by getting on her programme. By the end of the meal I could easily have written a 20 page story about her family, pets and hobbies. This is the way it should be. This is an invaluable opportunity to get to know a prospective buyer and if it is a previous customer, to ask about her family, job and hobbies.

9.   Where there are two men and one woman, avoid the danger of talking man to man and excluding the woman from the conversation.

I know a 30-year old unmarried woman executive who arranges large financial deals through banks for her company. The banks vie with each other for her business and sometimes invite her and one of her male colleagues to lunch. At one lunch there was the banker, her colleague (both about her age) and herself.

Both wives of the men had just had babies. The two men spent a large part of the lunch talking about their emotions when they were present at the birth of their respective babies – a total lack of empathy. They may have thought that *all* women are interested in childbirth. If so, they do not know the modern woman of today. She was bored.

10.   More and more people use first names nowadays. This is something I do myself but not generally at a first meeting unless she says 'Why not call me Jane?' or, if I sense the moment is right to say 'Why not call me Melvyn?'. Even if this is suggested, a new business acquaintance may not use your first name and some buyers will deliberately refrain from doing so. When they do start to use your name this is a sales signal that the luncheon is progressing satisfactorily.

One mistake that is often made by men when they are entertaining women executives is to shorten their name, a practice they very rarely do when they are entertaining a male customer. This has been confirmed in my research for this book by women. When there is a man and a woman together, some men will call the other man (who may work for the woman) Christopher, and never Chris. But Jacqueline becomes Jacky over lunch. One woman executive told me that men often abbreviate her name, Beverley, to Bev and she hates it.

The day after I wrote this I was taken out to lunch by Diane Needham, a PR expert. She said that male business executives often shorten her name to Di. Her friends never do. If you want to lose a client or customer never do this, unless she says 'Please call me Di'.

Women Entertaining
When a woman is entertaining in a sales situation most of the points made to date in this book are applicable. A few additional points are as follows:

11.   It is much more difficult for women executives to research the right kind of restaurants which they consider are ideal for their

business entertaining. Head waiters and restaurant staff are accustomed to dealing with female customers. They are less used to female executives – women who book a table, pay the bill even when they are with a man, and are working as they eat. Often without realising it, restaurant staff will give better service to a male customer.

Many waiters, or their parents, come from countries which are more dominated by men than our society, for example, Italy, Spain, Greece. Unless they are trained out of this attitude by management, they may treat women executives in the wrong way without realising it. Even British born staff can do the same. Many head waiters have agreed when we have discussed the subject. This is what happens.

When a woman arrives at the door of the dining room on her own, the head waiter automatically assumes that she is going to be joined by a man. If the head waiter is at another table, he will let her wait to see if she is joined by a man. He may only keep her waiting for a few seconds, but to the woman standing at the entrance it can seem years.

I was in a Glasgow hotel where the restaurant staff are very good. Mid-week in the evening, the restaurant usually has a number of business executives dining on their own. I counted 17 tables with just one person having dinner. Three were women – two were seated near the door, and one right by the exit door from the kitchen. The restaurant was fairly busy around 7.30 p.m. I discussed this with the restaurant manager. He looked around the room and said it was an accident, depending on who came in first.

The general manager took me round the hotel later and we went into the same restaurant to eat at 9.30 p.m. There was a new set of guests seated in the restaurant although it was only half full at this time, so there were plenty of tables available. The majority were business executives seated alone at their own tables. Two were women – one seated alone in the middle of the room, the other was seated at the awful table near the exit door from the kitchen.

Unintentionally or not, I do not believe that women executives are seated in the sequence they come in. This may lose me some friends in the restaurant world but I have seen this happen in many restaurants all over the country. In some restaurants women executives are seated in 'Outer Mongolia'!

Where this happens, steel yourself to be tough and complain quietly to the most senior person in the room, who may not necessarily be the person who shows you to a table. Try to do it quietly, firmly and with a smile. Be quietly assertive rather than aggressive.

If they look polite and are apologetic, but their eyes are glazed and they obviously do not know why you are making a fuss, then cross them off your list for future business entertaining. Someone has to sit near the kitchen, someone has to sit right near the entrance. But when you are selling, trying to create goodwill, or pull off a big deal, make sure that someone is someone else. When you are entertaining on business *you* may not mind a bad table but your prospective customer deserves the best table you can obtain.

12.   So strike off these unhelpful restaurants from your list. You now have a likely list and want to establish two (or three) to eat in regularly. You want to become someone who is recognised and treated as a regular. But the restaurant already has a lot of regulars and nowadays they are usually men, although this will change within five years.

Again, you have to try them out first. When you have chosen your most likely restaurant the only way I know to get yourself higher on the priority list is to introduce yourself to the owner or restaurant manager, either around noon or 3.00 p.m. when he has time to chat (as mentioned previously in Chapter 3).

Tell him your name, your position and company – and that you could be entertaining on business regularly in the future. I find the best way to phrase it is to say, with a smile 'It doesn't matter whether I get bad service and the worst table in the restaurant, but it is very, very important that my business guest receives good service and the best table available'. Give him your card and ask for his name. The first time you reserve a table (generally by telephone) ask to speak to him and remind him of your conversation. He will then reserve a good table, tell the staff, and the service should be fine. If it isn't, continue looking elsewhere.

13.   Assuming everything went well on your first visit, the second time you reserve a table do not necessarily ask for the restaurant manager again. It should not be necessary. He has to deal with as many customers as possible and does not like being 'hogged'.

14.   When you first talk to him do not tip him then. Some people do, but I explain why I do not recommend this in the separate chapter on Tipping.

15.   Where a restaurant is part of a hotel, it could be that you have had a quiet chat with the restaurant manager and you still do not receive the right level of attention and service. You may be located in a town, where that particular restaurant is much more suitable for business entertaining than others.

In that case, go and see the general manager of the hotel. Make an appointment and stress that you do not wish to see him to complain, but because you want to give him your business. He will see you, have a quiet word with the restaurant manager, and you should get the required level of service from then on.

16.   When women are entertaining on business, you will often find that the waitress, waiter (or the wine waiter if there is one) will present the wine list to the man at the table. This often arises even if the woman has booked in her name. The restaurant manager may know this when he shows you to the table, but he does not communicate to the waiter that you are doing the entertaining. So it is difficult to criticise the waiter. By acting quickly you must politely make sure that *you* are handed the wine list.

17.   Similarly, time after time, I have seen the waiter pour out the wine for tasting in the man's glass, almost as if women know nothing about wine and all men are experts. It is not necessarily a bad thing to let your guest taste the wine but he may not have seen the wine list and know exactly what you ordered. He may know

nothing about wine. Politely you have to correct the waiter so that you taste the wine.

18.   Make sure you ask for the bill and that the bill is presented to you and not your male guest. Many restaurants automatically present the bill to the man sitting at the table which can cause slight embarrassment if he is your customer. I try to get my restaurant clients to train staff so that they always present the bill to the right person and, if they are not sure, to place it in the centre of the table.

19.   Entertaining someone you have entertained many times before is a far easier situation than entertaining a customer or prospective customer for the first or second time. Many female executives have told me that it is more difficult to entertain another woman for the first time, rather than a man. The same people who say this rarely have a simple reason. They just smile and say 'Well you know what women are like when they are buying' Well I don't.

I think that a lot of this is imagination. Except where the luncheon is primarily the creation or continuation of goodwill, entertaining a strange person for the first time is no worse for a female entertaining a female than entertaining a male.

20.   One major point to consider is on the choice of location. There are many restaurants where women like to go together on a social basis. As an example, some women like Italian restaurants because the staff are more fun and certainly more attentive when there are two (or more) women eating out on a social basis. You must decide whether this style of restaurant is better for your own sales situation and the particular customer.

The same restaurant could be a disaster for entertaining a man/ woman on *business*. Business is a much more serious situation although it can still be relaxed and enjoyable. When you are involved in a soft sell situation you want to hold your customer's attention. You want to be able to make key sales points at various times during the meal period. This means that the buyer's attention must be on you and not on the activity of the restaurant. A restaurant with quiet but attentive staff is usually better for the first meal. The other kind of more social restaurant may be better for entertaining an out of town visitor over dinner.

*   *   *   *   *

You can see from these comments that women executives who entertain in a goodwill/sales situation can have a more difficult time than men in a restaurant.

Some get very angry about this and many have raged on about it to me. To be frank, it cannot be regarded as a continuous battle. The female executive must look upon it as a re-education process for a large number of restaurants who are used to dealing with male executives. Try some of the points made in this chapter. If you like a particular restaurant but they always give the wine list to your male guest, quietly re-educate them. Better still, buy an extra copy of this book and give it to them to read.

Gradually the situation for female executives will change. The sheer economics of market changes will force restaurant owners and staff to give equal attention to them. By the end of this decade, I believe that half the business of the restaurant trade will come from women executives entertaining. This means that restaurants who do not recognise the change could go out of business.

6

Entertaining Foreigners in this Country

Another complete book could be written on entertaining foreigners on business. But this book assumes readers have some experience and knowledge on this subject and therefore just covers the main key points. This aspect on foreigners is subdivided into two chapters covering the entertaining of foreigners in this country, and the entertaining of foreigners when you are abroad.

1. Generally in this book I am covering a situation where you can help to improve your technique when you are entertaining someone to whom you are endeavouring to sell. It does not generally cover the different emphasis when you are dealing with an executive who is selling to you and you are buying.

In the case of a foreigner (non resident of this country) who is selling to you, there is a strong case for entertaining him rather than the other way round. This may be costly and it will take time, but it could well create goodwill with a foreign supplier of a product and services, which could be important at some time in the future. In particular, when you have agreed a deal or a contract with a foreign supplier I would always recommend that he is entertained by you, assuming that there is sufficient time. It is not only good manners but also good business.

2. Our business lives are built round a discipline of waking at a certain time, eating at a certain time and working at a certain time. One of the problems with foreign visitors is that very often they

wake, eat and sleep at different times. It is difficult to adjust your own eating and work pattern to fit in with foreign visitors. Usually this isn't necessary because they will understand the situation as they are abroad. But it is important to be aware of the difference and, if you believe it is essential, adjust your time-table to their eating habits.

As examples, many Americans eat lunch and dinner earlier than we do. I have been invited to dinner, in America, at 5.30 p.m. and we sat down to eat at 5.45 p.m. Similarly, I have been invited to dinner in Spain at 9.00 p.m. and we did not eat until 10.30 p.m. The best thing to do is to show your awareness of the problem by asking. 'I know that Americans often eat early but I was planning to break for lunch at 12.30. Is this alright with you?'

3.   Whatever the eating times and habits of different r.ationalities, there is one common problem we all experience – jet lag and time differences. If your foreign visitor has travelled a long distance through time zones, his stomach may be at a totally different time of the day. Executives who travel are aware of this and do not expect other people to adjust their meal periods to fit in with them. But I have often found that clients are very grateful if you recognise this factor.

With a simple calculation, you can work out whether they have missed a meal and probably are hungry. If so, you can arrange for them to have a sandwich mid-morning with their coffee. Most offices are set up to make a simple sandwich or to send out for one. This kind of attention can create goodwill because it shows you are considerate. Alternatively, you may decide to go to lunch earlier than usual if he is feeling hungry.

I do not believe it is necessarily the amount of money you spend on entertaining but the way you do it. Arranging a snack or sandwich for an executive who is hungry is all part of business entertaining.

4.   Status is terribly important with many foreigners – points like who eats with them and where they sit. It is even important with many nationalities to make sure that the people who entertain

them are at a similar executive level. Foreign potential buyers should not be entertained by a lower status executive. With some nationalities (for example, Japanese) it would be a mistake to entertain them with an executive who is much higher than their level in their own country.

Many nationalities have more respect for their immediate boss and treat their company chairman or chief executive with a kind of awe. On a number of occasions I have seen a sales situation with a potential foreign buyer where the selling and negotiating is carried out by the buyer's peers but the company chairman entertains them for lunch. Many people have argued that this is a pleasant gesture and shows how hospitable the company is.

I have spoken to a number of foreigners who have been entertained in this situation and I am convinced that in the majority of cases it is a mistake. The chairman of the company is usually much older and it places the potential customer in a difficult situation which he does not quite know how to cope with. It is far better, if it can be arranged, for the chairman to join the people involved (sometimes there is a small team of people) just for drinks before lunch. I know of one chief executive who joins the luncheon party to say 'Hello' and has a cup of coffee towards the end of the meal.

5.   Where there is more than one person involved in having lunch, there is often a tendency for the waiter to seat people round a table in order to be helpful. He may not know the status and level of the different people involved. So it is important that you make sure that the key decision maker in the sales situation is given the best seat.

6.   Some larger companies who have a number of visitors from abroad (or other parts of Britain) and the conversation over lunch is not going to be private, decide to mix a group of people together, either in a restaurant or in their own in-house dining room. Sometimes this works and it can make a very pleasant relaxed luncheon between the sales situation during the day. But often it does not work especially when the visitor does not speak very good English. You may find he will gradually fade into the background.

It can sometimes be a disaster with some nationalities. I remember an occasion when a major factory, who exported a significant part of their production, had a group of Koreans and a group of Japanese visiting the factory.

The managing director decided to hire a small room at a local restaurant and organise a superb lunch asking both parties to join him. He never made the same mistake again. Neither the Koreans nor the Japanese, who by themselves are normally friendly and talkative, said a word throughout the whole luncheon. Some nationalities just do not mix.

7. If you are meeting a foreigner in a restaurant in order to entertain him, it is even more important to explain very clearly just how to get there and where to meet on arrival at the restaurant.

8. Wherever possible, pick them up by taxi or car, or send a car to pick them up. It is preferable for you to do this personally.

9. If you belong to one of the major clubs then take them there to eat. This usually makes a tremendous impression on foreigners. If it is convenient, spend half an hour taking them round the club or the rooms you can obtain access to with a visitor, and explain its background or history.

10. In our capital cities and main provincial towns many restaurants and hotels, have a history which could interest a foreigner. I know one provincial restaurant with a priest's bolt-hole. Foreigners love having this pointed out to them.

Hoteliers and restaurateurs neglect telling their customers more about the history of their premises; the famous (and infamous) people who have eaten there, or the well known owners and chefs of the restaurant. If the restaurant owners do not explain this, then it is interesting to tell a foreigner when you take him there for the first time. This may bore you, because you have told it many times, but your visitor will be fascinated. When they return home they are likely to tell their wives and other executives about it.

11. If your visitor is staying overnight, check that everything is

well with his hotel. If it is possible, and he is staying more than one night, then do something about it if he has problems.

12.   Usually business entertaining involves taking people out to lunch. With a foreigner who is staying at a hotel, it is a gesture to take him out for dinner, but check whether he is suffering from jet lag, feels tired, or wishes to have an early night.

13.   There is nothing more lonely than spending the whole day with people and finding that you are alone in a hotel in a strange city. It is also not always a pleasant experience to go down to the restaurant on your own and sit at a table on your own. So in a sales situation, it is important that you arrange to entertain your visitors in the evening, unless they are extremely tired.

14.   Where the visitor has been to your town before, try to take them out of town rather than to another restaurant in the same town or city. But do not take them too far so that there is a long drive back to their hotel afterwards. You want your prospective foreign customer to be well rested and receptive to your sales approach the next morning.

15.   There is another chapter in this book which deals with entertaining prospective buyers at home. Where a buyer is staying in your town or city overnight, and the situation is appropriate, try to take them home at least once on the trip. When executives are abroad and have spent a lot of time staying in hotels, there is nothing nicer than seeing the inside of a foreigner's home. This is elaborated in Chapter 10.

7

Entertaining when you are Abroad

This section does not go into all the detail of selling abroad. You should have briefed yourself fully before you make what is usually an expensive sales trip abroad, and in many companies, the most experienced traveller to that country will be sent on such a trip.

1. Culture shock can be a very real problem, particularly on your first visit to a country. Find out as much as possible about local customs and habits before the trip. It is possible to obtain a number of publications for exporters and people earning foreign currency, which outline what you can or cannot do in various foreign countries. These are published by the export divisions of the Department of Trade and Industry. A number of the major banks with branches in many countries also publish very useful booklets on the subject.

It is important to read these booklets and to ask a number of questions of anyone who has been to that country, before you go. Many people who are experienced in visiting a particular country will not tell you the most obvious things because they just take them for granted.

As an example, in some parts of America they seem surprised if you suggest taking them out for a very good lunch. They may be just as happy to grab a quick hamburger, if they are short of time. This is often the case in New York where everyone seems to disappear out of Manhattan around 5.00 p.m. They work a busy day and just do not have the time to have a lengthy lunch. Often they would prefer to talk business over a quick meal. In other parts of America, like San Francisco, they pride themselves on their restaurants and insist you have lunch every day.

Another example is in Nigeria. I remember leaving the office with a chief executive in order to have lunch just across the road. I suggested it would be nice to walk there, primarily because I like walking and had been sitting down all morning. This was met with a stony look. The chief executive insisted that his chauffeur drive us the 100 yards to the restaurant. With hindsight, I now realise that the chief executive had worked all his lifetime to obtain that chauffeur and that car, and he was going to use it. Lower status people walk! I would hazard a guess that within ten years the status symbol in Nigeria for executives may well be jogging. But being driven by a chauffeur is the status symbol now. You must find out as much as possible about this kind of point before you go.

2.   Even if you are selling, you will often find that people abroad will entertain you over lunch and dinner. They may be positively insulted by your suggestion that you take them out for a meal, even when you want their business. If they wish to take you out, do not argue with the situation or mention it again when the bill arises.

3.   The guide lines and points mentioned on choosing the right venue should you be doing the entertaining, are the same as set out in Chapter 3. The only problem is that very often you haven't the time to research and choose a venue which is most suitable and where you are well known. Ask before you go. It is quite likely that you will be given the names of two or three restaurants by other executives who have been there before.

4.   If this is not the case, use published restaurant guides, if available. They will often give you the widest degree of choice, and a good indication of the type of menu and service. One major advantage of using a guide when you are entertaining abroad is that if the restaurant turns out to be a disaster, you can always blame the guide!

5.   In some countries where there are no guides and very few proper restaurants, ask the air cabin crew for some suggestions.

6.   Depending on the style of hotel you are using, you could eat in the hotel restaurant. This at least will give you a chance to look at the menu beforehand and to talk to the headwaiter and staff. In many developing countries it is safer to eat in the hotel restaurant, from a security and a health point of view.

7.   If you are still undecided where to take your customer to eat, then the best thing is to explain the situation to him and ask him for any suggestions.

8.   When you are entertaining abroad (and this may also arise in Britain) make sure that the restaurant you choose accepts your credit cards. If necessary, phone beforehand. There is nothing more embarrassing than your client having to pick up the tab if you do not have sufficient cash.

I once entertained a very important banker in San Francisco and he suggested that we had a meal in the best Japanese restaurant in town. At the end of the meal, to my amazement, I found they did not accept credit cards – something I hadn't noticed beforehand.

9.   Often when you are selling abroad, people will invite you home in the evening and perhaps over the weekend. This will more often arise if the deal is fairly large. So it does become a key sales situation. This also makes foreign travel particularly interesting. I have been invited home in the major countries, but also in places as different as Mbane, Swaziland, Kano in Northern Nigeria, and Curepipe in Mauritius.

Always take a small gift, even if it is just flowers or chocolates. Sometimes this is difficult because the buyer suddenly says 'Let me take you home for a drink and dinner' and you are already in his car. It is important to insist politely that you stop somewhere so that you can buy a gift for his wife or children. There are some countries where it is unimportant if you bring a gift or not. But this gesture is of key importance in many others.

10. In many places it is a mistake to take along a bottle of drink as we might do in this country. This would apply not only to those countries where religion forbids the drinking of alcohol, but also in other societies. But in other countries, e.g. Israel or Ireland a bottle of brandy or whisky off the plane would be looked on favourably.

11. Don't always expect to get a drink, because some societies just do not drink, even if there is no religious ruling against this. As an example, I have worked in Israel on a few occasions where we have had the most marvellous meal and never had any alcohol. On one accasion, when we finished the meal, I was asked whether I would like a drink. 'Yes' I replied with delight. I was then brought coffee!

Similarly, in some Arab countries I have consumed more alcohol than I would do normally. It all depends on the circumstances. You have to be totally flexible when you are selling abroad.

12. When you are in your potential customer's home, do not sell or talk business unless *he* brings up the subject first. This point is even more important if he asks you to come home during a weekend or on a national holiday. He is off work and enjoying himself and it is important that you do exactly the same.

13. Do not always expect to be introduced to the wife. I have had dinner in many Muslim countries where I have not seen the wife throughout the whole evening although I have been introduced to the children. There are other countries where I have been introduced to her at the end of the meal.

14. Generally the wife will be together with you when you eat. In my opinion, she is the key person in the sales situation. I do not believe that she is the decision-maker unless she has some working role in the company, but she can often be a decision-maker in a negative sense by turning your prospective customer off you and your whole sales approach.

It is vitally important to talk to her even if your hobbies, interests and work may be more akin to those of the husband. When you talk to her, ask her questions about herself, her children and her hobbies. Nowadays, many more married women work and there will be a growing number of occasions in the future where you are invited home where the man and the woman are not married, or both are working.

In one city I was invited home by a man, and his partner was another man. No prizes for guessing that this was San Francisco. If the wife (or partner) approves, then you are a little further along the road to a successful sales situation.

15.   It is a very personal decision but – apart from some Muslim countries – I feel many married men miss out when they are selling abroad by not taking their wives with them, even when she doesn't work and the children are older. You will be entertained and socialised much more if they know in advance that your wife is coming with you. If you brief your wife fully on your objectives, the cost will be repaid handsomely in increased contracts and sales. Apart from the financial benefits it will certainly make your wife's life more interesting.

8

Entertaining the Press

At some stage in your business activity or career, you will have to entertain the press. Many executives deliberately establish a relationship with specific reporters. You may want to obtain some free press publicity for your particular product, services or your financial results.

It could be that you are just entertaining a particular journalist or reporter as part of your PR campaign. This means that when you do have a specific story, you can ring that particular person, and receive a more favourable reaction thus improving your chances of obtaining more coverage than if you entertained him only when you have a specific story.

This chapter is not a treatise on PR generally but only on some key aspects with regard to entertaining the press. There are a growing number of women journalists working for the national, local and trade press. Therefore, key points in Chapter 5 should be considered.

Virtually every journalist has one common problem – this is that they all work to a deadline. Sometimes the deadline is monthly, sometimes weekly, often daily.

Even when a reporter works for a monthly magazine, there will be an intense pressure period and a deadline towards the end of the month. This is not because they leave everything to the last moment but because they want news and stories to be as fresh as possible. The printing process creates another deadline and a further stress situation.

All kinds of PR and business entertaining has to recognise that many journalists are very short of time until they get their story in, when quite naturally they relax. Therefore, some key points in helping you maximise results from press entertaining are as follows.

1.   If the journalist is on a daily newspaper make sure that you try to choose a restaurant which is within a short taxi ride or walk of his work which, in London, is generally Fleet Street.

2.   Before you choose a restaurant to entertain the press, check out the telephone situation. Some restaurants do not have a real public telephone. Try to find one with two public telephones because there is nothing worse for a journalist to find that someone is using the only telephone when he is trying to send in his story.

When this happens, do not hesitate to ask the restaurant owner whether your guest – the journalist – can use his personal telephone. If you have established a personal relationship with the owner and staff, this should not be a problem – they will be delighted to help. He may not want to telephone a story on your activities, but he may have come from a meeting or press conference direct to your luncheon and has to telephone directly after lunch.

3.   Try to use a restaurant where the public telephones are in a fairly private place and not necessarily near the restaurant where the background noise might be high. Obviously this privacy is of critical importance if you are dealing with any aspect of your company which might influence the stock market.

4.   Many restaurants within hotels are well equipped with public telephones. So are many restaurants within specialist function rooms.

5.   Ask beforehand how much time they have. Make sure that they have sufficient time for deadlines. If you know the journalist, tell him when you fix the lunch date that you have a news story or that it is just for a general chat.

6.   Have your story and message typed with appropriate photographs (if applicable) in an envelope with you at the table and not left in your briefcase in the cloakroom. A lot of executives do not like cluttering the table with briefcases and envelopes, but it is necessary for a number of reasons – one of them being that they may have to leave suddenly (see point 10).

7.   When you have the package with you some journalists may ask for the story before you start to eat so that they can then relax, and if necessary telephone the story immediately. This is ideal in many respects but you must control the situation.

8.   I have known journalists to reach out and 'grab' the package. Do not let them do this. Only hand over your PR package after you have given a verbal run down to stimulate his interest first. If he is not on a daily or has a deadline, give your verbal run down after he has finished the main course, preferably around dessert/coffee time. Do not leave this too late.

9.   Try to choose a restaurant with fairly large tables so that he can write. There are many excellent restaurants around with small tables. At some stage the journalist may well wish to write and take notes. There is nothing more inconvenient than trying to do this in between cups and saucers, or on his knee.

10.   The journalist may well wish to leave early even though he has not mentioned this at the start of the meal. Be prepared for this, so do not leave your key points until the very end of the brandies and cigars.

11.   If your story is sufficiently interesting, many journalists may decide to leave you after the main course and telephone the story there and then. Often they will then return to the table. If they do this it is an extremely good sign.

12.   Some journalists like to drink and why not. As mentioned earlier, they lead a pressured existence. With empathy *and* sympathy you should recognise this and be prepared for them to drink.

13.   The journalist may stay longer than you thought. Once he has telephoned his story in, this is the point where he can stop working and relax, and you can establish a personal relationship.

14.   If you are entertaining the press, always arrange with your office that you will not have another appointment until after 3.00 p.m. If you get back earlier fine. Always allow much more time for entertaining the press over lunch than you would do for other people.

*   *   *   *   *

Obtaining free press publicity is one of the most cost effective ways of promoting your products, services, and creating a certain image for your company. You may have to adjust your own eating habits and time schedule to fit in with theirs because they are important. The press work different and, in many ways, much longer hours than you do. It takes a lot of patience and time to build up a relationship with a number of key journalists. The foregoing list of points, read in conjunction with other relevant chapters, should help in this direction.

9

Entertaining in your own Premises (Factories, Offices, Banks)

A significant number of companies have their own in-house feeding facilities. Many large organisations have these for all grades of staff. Some companies will have a specific dining room for directors or other executives when a luncheon is required and a discussion needs to be private.

Nearly every bank in the City of London has private dining rooms to entertain visitors. Most large office complexes and factories have them and some large departmental stores have this kind of facility. In the larger Marks and Spencer departmental stores there is usually a room off the general staff restaurant so that the manager can entertain visitors. Most of the larger firms of accountants and solicitors have dining rooms in their offices.

In many cases when a luncheon is held the reason is a kind of selling. Some professional people say that this is not so. But virtually every situation of in-house entertaining has an element of creating goodwill and this, to my mind, is selling. There are still sections of British society who believe that there is something wrong in 'selling', but this is changing rapidly. Some banks may not call it selling, but for years they have been in the business of selling their services. Many merchant banks have done this very efficiently.

I have eaten at Rothschild, Hill Samuel, Orion Royal and numerous other banks. Some of the finest food I have had, has been at these luncheons, and the same comment certainly applies to the wines. It is interesting to note that when you are invited to lunch at a bank in this country invariably you will be offered wine. If you are invited to a bank in America you will often have a superb meal but in many cases they will not offer you wine with the meal.

On one visit to the Ford Motor factory in Detroit, when it came to lunch time the top executives asked me if I would join them. Of course I said 'Yes' and we then walked to the restaurant, joined a line (queue), picked up our trays with everyone else, and collected our meal. They had what is called single status dining in this large factory. We then sat at tables which were exactly the same as everyone else but slightly isolated from the general area, so that we could have a more private discussion. This single status dining saves a significant amount in wage costs, and space costs generally. Compare this to the situation in the United Kingdom where, in one large factory, I counted nine different grades of staff restaurants.

The major difference between in-house feeding and entertaining someone in a normal restaurant is that the commercial aspect is taken out of the situation. You do not receive a menu with prices, do not receive a bill and naturally you do not have to pay.

The other major difference in having your own top executive in-house feeding facility is that it has to be extremely good. If something goes wrong you cannot blame the restaurant. Some in-house restaurants are run by the company's own experts in food management and others are run by 'outside' contract caterers. Usually in the top executive dining rooms where there is entertainment of outside visitors, there is incredible attention to detail.

Here are some further suggestions and points to watch when using your own facilities.

1.   Many experienced businessmen do not mind going to a strange restaurant, but feel nervous about eating in a top executive or directors' dining room. I remember the first time I was invited to lunch at Rothschild at New Court in the City of London. I was arranging a major merger between two British hotel companies. Rothschild was the merchant bank involved.

I was waiting in reception and casually asked the porters on duty why they did not have the name of the bank outside but just had the words New Court. The porter said to me in a very nice way 'Rothschild never put their name outside their premises. They do not need to'.

As I was directed to a dining room I became more and more overawed by a sense of history. So I can quite understand why many business visitors find that having lunch at a merchant bank in the City of London is a slightly nerve wracking experience. It is very important for bankers to realise this. The same point applies to many director's dining rooms.

2.   The visitor should not be shown into a room and left on his own. Bankers are pressured people and it is quite common for them to arrive late after the visitor has arrived. This has happened to me. I would suggest that a host is available who can welcome people, show them to the room, pour them a drink and wait for a few moments until one of the bank executives arrives. I would say that on one out of every three occasions I have been shown into a room, and then left waiting. Naturally, when people do arrive they are very apologetic and charming, but I believe it should not happen.

3.   Sometimes someone is late and everybody waits for that person to arrive. This is not just the case with banks but more so in certain factory and head office dining rooms. Often you have to wait for the most senior person to arrive before you can eat, even though a major buyer may be present.

4.   I have *never* been asked if there is any food that I do not particularly like and sometimes the choice is limited, even though the food is excellent. I once attended a luncheon with a colleague who was allergic to shell fish, and lobster was on the menu.

5.   These luncheons are rarely a one to one situation. Quite often the person you are seeing invites along some colleagues. Generally this means that you have to address yourself to a number of people throughout the luncheon. Often the dining table is quite long. I am sure that readers will appreciate that if you are sitting in the wrong

place this could mean that you have to swivel your head the whole
time.

I would suggest that the visitor is placed at one end of the table
and not in the middle. I thought it was nice when the chief executive
of a major company suggested that I sat in his chair at the head of
the table. I found out afterwards that he always does this.

6.   Please remember that you may know the system involved, but the visitor may not. If there is a degree of self help, it is important to explain this. Often a very quiet butler is employed who is chosen for his discretion, as the conversation can have some extremely important private or financial implications. This type of waiter can be very quiet. Only recently I was having lunch in a director's dining room, and I wondered why everybody was staring at me. I continued talking and no one said a word, but glancing around I saw that the waiter was standing to my left just behind me, I had not noticed him or heard him come up.

7.   When you have a situation which is not one to one, and the visitor is normally outnumbered, *you* will have plenty of time to eat when you are not talking. But the visitor may have to answer questions from three or four people. So please bear this in mind and give him time to eat.

8.   These luncheons normally end on time, usually at 2.30 p.m. in banks, or at 2.00 p.m. in factories and offices. If a visitor is on his first visit, and not necessarily buying a specific product at the end of the meal, offer to show him round the factory or the offices. I found it very interesting looking behind the scenes at a Marks and Spencer store. I have also been shown round breweries. When I was eating at the head office of Shell on the Embankment, I was surprised when they showed me round, to see the facilities they had for staff in the way of a swimming pool and gymnasiums.

Many banks cannot show visitors round their entire premises for obvious reasons but there are certain parts, like the foreign exchange sections, which visitors find interesting. I have usually found most factory activities worth seeing, particuarly when there is a new form of automation. There is one tour operator who runs a holiday type tour to Japan and on the itinerary are visits round Japanese factories. Often, after a good lunch, we perhaps neglect the opportunity to show off our facilities and products, unless the person is purchasing a specific product.

9.   If you are dining on the top floor of an office block the views can be interesting, even spectacular. It is worthwhile pointing out

well known landmarks to visitors from abroad, or out of town. You see them every day, but a visitor does not.

On the ninth floor of a leading bank's premises they pointed out St. Paul's Cathedral to me. I am not sure why they then pointed out the Old Bailey, but I didn't take this personally! After a lunch in a high rise office in New York I was given a scroll photograph of the view as a memento. These little touches turn a good meal into an experience you do not forget. It certainly improves goodwill.

10

Entertaining Executives at Home

Entertaining at home on business is the trickiest of all entertaining situations. If successful, it can go a long way to creating goodwill with your client or customer. I have known situations where the customer has made up his mind only after seeing the person in his home environment.

Often the decision to sign a contract or place an order with you or your competitor could go either way. Many kinds of selling do not just involve the service or product, but also selling yourself.

So be prepared if you invite someone home. Your home is an extension of yourself and can be a critical factor in making a favourable impression. Experienced readers, who have entertained at home for years, will understand many of the comments made below. Entertaining at home socially with friends is totally different to entertaining at home on business.

Many of the points made before on entertaining in a restaurant are not valid with regard to eating at home except for the major ones of pre-preparation and setting objectives. Often when entertaining at home, the objective is just to get your client to relax and to create goodwill.

1.   If you have been entertaining at home for years and are very experienced, fine. But if you are thinking of starting to entertain at home, then my advice is *don't*. Or at least question and reconsider the whole situation. Many executives suddenly think that it would be an extremely good idea to entertain at home. But this good idea can often turn into a near nightmare.

2.   You have to ask yourself a whole series of questions and you must be very honest with your replies. How experienced is your wife or partner in entertaining people she has never or rarely seen before? How good is her cooking? How good is her presentation of food at the table – which is as important as the quality of her cooking? Does she work? Is your wife (or partner) experienced at meeting people, or does she tend to get nervous and tense? You have to ask yourself, quite honestly, whether you are going to cause her problems. Should you burden her with the whole problem? Will she enjoy acting as a hostess?

3.   Where you are a female executive thinking of entertaining someone at home, you have to ask similar questions about your husband or partner. Even the question of cooking may be relevant. More women work away from home, and some men have jobs where they work from home and do the cooking.

In other cases, the wife's working role means that she arrives home much later than the man and he tends to do the cooking. Nowadays, it is not just a question of wives playing a supportive role for their husbands, although this is still important for the majority of people, but also a situation where the husband plays a supportive role to his wife, who may be earning more money than he is.

4.   Are your home facilities appropriate for entertaining? You do not necessarily have to impress your guest but you do have to ask yourself some very honest questions. As an example, many homes, particularly *new* houses, have small dining areas. When you are entertaining a number of visitors will you have the space?

5.   If you decide to entertain with some of your colleagues at your home, and there are one or more visitors, can your kitchen cope with the kind of meal you want to put on, bearing in mind the numbers involved?

Older houses tend to have large kitchens but some houses have a lack of working surfaces even if they have every conceivable appliance. Most home kitchens are designed to cater for up to six people for a full cooked meal. If there are more than six people there could be problems. You should consider a pre-prepared buffet if you must entertain more than six people.

6.   In earlier chapters it has been emphasised that before you choose a particular restaurant you should try it out beforehand. Some of the most successful entertaining I have seen at home, particularly by young executives and their wives, has been when they have tried the situation out beforehand by inviting one or two friends to carry out a dummy run of the whole menu, wines and meal experience.

7.   Often, the best arrangment is to take your visitor home for drinks and snacks and then to go out to a local restaurant for a meal. Your partner is going to be more relaxed in this situation. The same point may well apply to you. The visitor will have a chance to see you in your home environment, possibly to see your children, and then enjoy the restaurant in a relaxed frame of mind. In this case make sure you have followed the procedures in Chapter 3 on Choosing a Restaurant.

8.   Some executives have their own staff at home. But the vast majority of people do not. You might well consider hiring a local caterer to cater for a small dinner party. In most local newspapers there are a number of people advertising this kind of service. In fact the number has grown considerably in the last few years. Many of the people who organise small dinner parties have professional qualifications.

Check what these qualifications are. The professional association for many hoteliers and caterers is the Hotel and Catering Institutional Management Association (HCIMA) with over 22,000 members.

9.   If you decide to have outside caterers prepare the meal, then invest in the time and money to try them out first before you use them on the all important evening. When you do use them on an experimental basis ask what their strengths and weaknesses are. You may find that one is expert at making pastries with a speciality for unusual desserts. If so, encourage them to do something special

for the night. Or they may know a lot about food but nothing about wine. It is important to find this out beforehand. Do not hesitate to ask for references, and telephone the referee to find out whether he/she was satisfied with the meal produced.

10.   Buy good wines for the evening and see they are served at the right temperature. Ensure you also have a good supply of different kinds of drinks. Do not leave it until the actual evening to check this out.

11.   As more people drink cocktails, it is worthwhile experimenting with some of the more unusual ones. It is important to break the ice early on by getting people to relax. I often suggest that people should invent their own cocktail (which is quite easy to do) as this can be a good opening talking point. But check first whether they like the base alcohol of the cocktail.

After years of travelling round the world and in America in particular, I finally learnt how to make a very dry Martini. When serving them I began to notice they were so dry that they were far too strong for most people. Americans may like them but other nationalities find them too dry.

12.   Check whether your visitor has any special food preferences, or is on a special diet.

13.   Remember that it is not an occasion for the man to relax while his wife works all the time. You cannot leave your guest during the evening to help your wife in the kitchen but, on the other hand, if you give her no assistance whatsoever things may go wrong and she will be less likely to want to give another party in the future.

14.   If your visitor is from abroad, or out of town, be prepared for him to stay overnight, even if this is not planned. Again, ask yourself a series of questions. Are the facilities in your house sufficient to cope with an extra person. Friends can 'muck in', a business visitor is different.

Do you have a mass exodus of people first thing in the morning as your children fight to get into the bathroom, before they grab breakfast and rush off to school or work, with you trying to fit your guest in around the same time. The added burden of an extra out of town visitor can create real problems. On the other hand, if you have an extra room then by all means put up your visitor for the night. Many businessmen who spend a lot of time travelling round the world staying in hotels, find it a pleasant experience to spend a night in a home.

15.   This is an occasion when you must get up early so that you are ready and prepared before your guest is. You may have to adjust the timetable of all the other members of the family to ensure that your guest gets into the bathroom without waiting and has an unpressured breakfast. In this way he will be in a pleasant receptive mood for your business activities during the day.

16.   Remember the entertaining does not stop at dinner. It includes breakfast the next morning. Ask whether your visitor wishes to have a cooked breakfast and check that you have a mixture of cereals and some bran based cereals. Where you have children, this can often be quite fun and many visitors enjoy this.

I remember an overnight visit, about ten years ago, by a Canadian executive, Daniel Sterfels, whose parents were French and he was brought up in Venezuela. His taste in food and eating was adventurous. He had never seen Marmite before and we all watched with fascination as he tried it out for the first time at breakfast.

As the years passed, I met him occasionally and he always remarked, 'Do you remember when I tried Marmite for the first time'? A week after writing this comment I received a postcard from Daniel to say he is Dean of the Hotel School of Catholic University in the Dominican Republic. Perhaps he only remembers me because of his experience with Marmite!

17.   If you are inviting the same executive home for more than one night, then I would suggest that you eat out on the second night, rather than repeat entertaining at home for the following evening.

18.   If you have an overnight client or customer from out of town or from abroad, then weekends are the finest opportunity to create goodwill. In this situation they can join in the family fun. Eating can be a far more relaxed situation with barbecues in the summer or buffets at other times of the year. One of my fondest memories is being invited to Sunday brunch by one of my associates, Jim Little in Toronto, when the grandparents were present as well. As a family man away from home, it was a heart-warming experience.

19.   Should you be inviting a customer home for Sunday lunch, and you have a local pub with character, then take them out to your local before lunch.

*   *   *   *   *

When the home entertaining is over, assess how well it went and whether you achieved your objectives. Do this constructively and critically, not to destroy your own confidence but in order to improve the situation the next time you invite a prospective customer home for a meal.

11

Entertaining your Bank Manager

It used to be unheard of to entertain bank managers. In fact, most of the major high street banks had a policy where bank managers were not entertained by clients.

However, in the last few years this embargo has been relaxed and I know a number of people who entertain their bank managers. When I mention this to other executives they seem faintly surprised as if it is quite a unique idea, and I believe that in many cases, it has never entered most executives minds. Recently I took my bank manager out to lunch. I mentioned this to ten executives. Only one of them said he had ever done this. He had his own restaurant where he entertained his bank manager.

The situation usually arises where the executive is self employed, or deals with the financing side of a major company. Here are some ideas and suggestions with regard to entertaining your bank manager, which should not be read in isolation from the previous chapters.

1.   Think carefully before you do so. He will make it very obvious whether in fact he wishes to have lunch with you or not, but you must not put him in a difficult situation by phrasing the invitation in such a way that he has to be blunt to refuse.

Say something like 'I know this is a particularly busy time of the year for you . . .'. This will give him an opportunity to either accept or refuse.

2.   Don't ask your bank manager out to lunch if you want to borrow money at that point of time. It would be a fatal mistake and could well backfire on you. Banks are in business to lend money but there is a time and a place to ask for it.

3.   There are many businesses where there are certain times of the year when cash flow is low and an overdraft is required, and other times when there is surplus cash flow. The time to take your bank manager out to lunch is when there is a surplus of cash flow. He will not forget the lunch (because not many people invite him) but it will create goodwill when you have to ask for an overdraft facility or a higher overdraft.

4.   If you have some good news, like a major order or contract, then use this as a reason to invite him out to lunch but do not tell him about it until you are actually having lunch. Just say you have some good news.

5.   Conversely, tell him very early on that you do not want to increase your overdraft facility. He will then relax and enjoy the meal experience.

6.   When you are having lunch up-date him about your business activities, but also ask his advice on other matters. Some bank managers in certain branches have a very varied life. Other bank managers have a more repetitive life where there is not much difference between the meetings with their various clients. Nowadays, bank managers are trained in modern management techniques, they are taught marketing, they read about unit trusts and know a lot about insurance policies.

So take the opportunity to ask his advice about a new insurance policy or whether you should sell some unit trusts. This will give him an opportunity to show you some of the knowledge he has acquired. Often he does not get a chance to talk about his management skills but spends most of his time listening to other people talking about themselves.

7.   Don't take him to the most expensive place in town. Think carefully where you take him. If you spend a fortune he may well

think that he indirectly is paying for that luncheon. So take him somewhere better than average but not to the type of restaurant where receiving the bill is described as breaking the bank.

8.   Do not arrange for an extensive, long luncheon. He may be able to arrange for a longer lunch break than normal but he may be short of time. Similarly you must show him that you haven't got hours to spend socialising, and you must get back to business at a certain time.

9.   Do not entertain your bank manager too regularly. Once or twice a year should be sufficient, bearing in mind you should be seeing him, or talking to him on the telephone throughout the year. You can establish a relationship, even a friendly relationship with him. Entertaining too often could be too 'obvious'.

*   *   *   *   *

In Chapter 1 I mentioned that whatever your feelings on the cost of social entertaining in restaurants, entertaining on business when you are selling or creating goodwill is an essential part of your overall expenditure, and a really good investment. Access to finance at the right time keeps all of our businesses healthy. It is vital if we experience recessions, and essential when we expand. Entertaining your bank manager could be the best investment you ever make.

12

Entertaining Stockbrokers

Many directors of companies quoted on the stock exchange have contact with stockbrokers. Many more directors whose companies are not quoted on the main stock exchanges but are thinking of bringing their companies to the Unlisted Securities Market are beginning to have contact with stockbrokers.

Stockbrokers do a considerable amount of entertaining. They are probably the most sales orientated group of people I know. Unashamedly they sell, but always in a nice warm, open manner. Being entertained by a stockbroker is always fun as well as being good business. I have never been entertained without the lunch involving serious discussion about business.

On occasions I have addressed representatives of financial institutions about the hotel industry at luncheons given by various firms of stockbrokers. Although I found the situation quite exacting, I always enjoyed the meal and ambience.

Many stockbrokers do the entertaining themselves and it is rare to have to entertain them. But senior company directors, and many major shareholders in companies, are beginning to invite stockbrokers to have lunch with them. It is a good policy to take the stockbrokers out of their usual environment to dine in your premises, or your usual restaurant.

Here are some points to consider if you are planning to entertain your own stockbroker or a stockbroker you may plan to use in the future.

1. Find out who the people are in the research departments of the stockbroker. Always include them in the invitation. Generally it is essential to do your own 'selling' to the partners or executives who work in the research departments – what I would call the intelligence service.

2. You usually have to entertain more than one person. There could be one or two people from the research department and one other general partner. So be prepared to be outnumbered by sometimes three or four to one. Some people tell me that they even up the numbers by bringing along some of their own executives in order to show they are part of a team. Other chief executives entertain on their own in order to put across a specific message.

It is not a negotiating situation where you have to have a team of people, but rather one where you are quietly trying to give an impression of confidence, without giving away confidential facts and figures.

3. Many research departments issue publications and specialise in a particular field or industry. If you are in this particular segment of industry you should entertain the stockbroking firm which specialises in published research projects on your field.

4. Quote from the report and ask them specific questions even if these are unrelated to any comments within that report about your own particular company. I know some people who work in these research departments. These researchers spend an enormous amount of time and effort producing the research documents. They always feel extremely flattered if the chief executive of the quoted company, or a senior executive of a non-quoted company, has taken the time to read their work and is prepared to ask some questions about it.

5. Very often, the senior executive of the company or major shareholder doing the entertaining, tends to be older than some of the stockbrokers. Try to avoid addressing comments to the more senior member. Make sure that equal attention and eye contact is paid to the whole team. The older person may not necessarily be the most influential person present.

6.   Match the style and level of their entertaining, which is high. Do not stint on good wines.

7.   Devote a certain amount of time to the lunch without, in any way hurrying them. Then ask for the bill when you are having coffee. Without rushing. leave shortly after signing the bill. I have spoken to many stockbrokers who have said that after being taken out to lunch last week by Mr XYZ, 'He seemed very relaxed but he certainly didn't waste any time over lunch and we left promptly as soon as we had finished coffee.' I have heard this comment many times and it obviously makes an impression on stockbrokers.

13

Tipping

Many people worry about tipping. Tipping is certainly a very complex situation in many restaurants. This chapter is not going to repeat the many arguments which appear in the press from time to time on this whole subject and whether to abolish tipping.

The same correspondence appears periodically in the correspondence columns of the hotel and catering press and it is a subject where most restaurateurs and members of the public have strong feelings – which all seem to differ. In my opinion, there is no doubt that tipping is going to be with us for a long, long time.

In a social eating situation it does not really matter if there is some confusion over tipping. People eating together socially can laugh about it. But it is a more delicate situation with regard to business entertaining, and the following points may well help to smooth your path in the future.

At present the situation is a jungle with so many variations that the public is bound to be confused. Examples of the variations are as follows:

Service Charge is included (but no amount is mentioned).

Service Charge is not included.

10% Service Charge is included.

10% Service Charge is included, and this is wholly distributed to the staff.

Service Charge is included and it is only necessary to tip for special services rendered.

Service Charge is included. Individual gratuities are discretionary.

Our staff receive a good market rate salary and therefore there is no need to tip.

There are many variations on the above. Some menus state nothing about tipping or service charge.

Many restaurant staff who look upon their job as a career, dislike the whole aspect of tipping. On the other hand, they are so used to it as part of the norm, that it really does not seem to worry them (like taxi drivers). In some countries there is virtually a law that you pay a certain percentage, for example 15 per cent in America. If you pay less in the way of a tip, they will soon let you know they are unhappy about this.

Most regular career restaurant staff I know, prefer an automatic service percentage added on, with a further additional tip only paid in special circumstances. The following are key points on tipping when you are entertaining on business.

1.   Check beforehand, so you know what the situation is in the way of service charge, and no confusion is likely to arise at the end of the meal period.

2.   If it is not possible to find out the tipping and service charge policy in advance, be sure that you read the small print at the bottom of the menu at the beginning of the meal.

What sometimes happens is that people say 'Let's skip dessert and have a quick cup of coffee'. At that point you want to get the bill and you have not seen the service charge policy written on the menu, because you no longer have the menu. Not all bills state the service charge policy and you may have to ask.

3.   Whatever the policy try to stick to it except under special circumstances. If the policy is to add on a 10 per cent service charge then do not increase this to 15 per cent except in special circumstances.

4.   Where the policy is not clear, ask at an appropriate time.

5.   When you decide to tip by adding on a 10 per cent service charge, try to round *up* the amount to an even sum. Often your potential client or customer may be watching. You see some people going through what appears to be a complex calculation in order to add on to a credit card slip, an *exact* 10 per cent service charge of £2.69. Better to round it up to £3.

6.   Try to tip in cash, if available.

7.   Some people who have a credit account give an instruction to the restaurant owner that the cashier should automatically add on a percentage service charge. I would not advise this because it is very easy for this to be accepted as the norm, and service may decline. It does not take long to add on an amount for service each time when you sign the bill.

8.   I have found that it never affects the service if I stick strictly to the policy laid down by the restaurant for tipping, except under special circumstances. As an example, not long ago I took out a client whose son had just received a high university degree. I knew about this beforehand and told the restaurant, so that we could have a good bottle of champagne ready to celebrate. The restaurant owner congratulated my client on his son's success (which pleased my client) and they gave us that little extra service, I showed my appreciation by giving them an additional tip.

9.   What I generally do is to keep to the service charge policy. Once a year I give an additional tip to the restaurants I use regularly, generally at Christmas, in an envelope. Most good restaurants have a system of allocating tips between the various grades of staff and it is not necessary to give special envelopes to a series of different waiters. Usually they will pool the total tip and it is distributed proportionately. In a well established restaurant, God help the employee who takes more than his agreed portion of the service charge and tips!

10.   I have seen some people, from time to time, give a tip or

present of the product they actually sell. This can make a very big impression. One restaurant manager told me that a regular client who manufactures perfume, brings in a package of his new lines when they are launched for the restaurant owner, and to give out to the staff.

I know a magazine publisher who gave out a free subscription to one of his family magazines, to the five top people running the restaurant. Naturally, if you are selling massive generators or financing international commodity deals, then it is not possible to give something in kind. But another executive I know who runs a small department store gives away at Christmas gift vouchers to the restaurant staff where he eats regularly.

I have given away copies of my previous management book, Marketing Hotels into the 90s, to the restaurants where I entertain regularly on business and to a number of other restaurant managers, where I eat on a social basis.

11.   When you are selling, tip discreetly. In discussing this with a number of executives they have argued the point that the other restaurant staff must see that you have tipped the head waiter, so that they are not excluded and do not neglect you on the next visit. Restaurant staff have a kind of secret antennae and they certainly know when other people have been tipped.

Restaurant management, and I do use the word management, are part of a profession. There may be some restaurant managers or staff who cheat on others when it comes to tipping, but the vast majority are hard working and honest. Although they are used to it, most of them do not necessarily like people who tip with a grand flourish. They will not give that person any less service but they will not necessarily give him any better service.

*   *   *   *   *

These points may help you on the complicated subject of tipping. Another advantage of staying with your regular tested restaurants is that there should be no confusion on the tipping situation.

14

Entertainment Expenses –
Allowable for Tax Purposes?

This chapter covers the tax situation on business entertaining in Great Britain. Readers in the Channel Islands, Isle of Man and other countries may find their own tax situation different.

1.   Generally speaking, entertainment expenses are not normally deductible unless in connection with overseas customers and their agents. The cost of entertaining your own staff is deductible. This is generally not realised by a number of people.

Therefore, if you are having a business meeting and decide to continue this over lunch with your own staff, this would be considered as a deductible item for tax purposes.

2.   When you are travelling on business either at home or abroad then the cost of your travel, hotel, meals and other expenses can be charged as subsistence or under the heading, 'travel and subsistence' and is deductible for tax purposes – it is not within the definition of entertainment.

3.   If it is vital for your business to research restaurants, then the cost incurred should be tax deductible. Many hoteliers, restaurateurs and other businessmen do not realise that this is the case. Similarly, it is conceivable that executives connected with the food industry, where their products end up as part of the meal in a restaurant, could properly claim that they are carrying out research when they are eating in that restaurant, and thus avoid being assessed under the benefit in kind provisions.

4.   Similarly, people connected with brewery and wine industries must keep abreast of market trends by eating (and drinking) in restaurants. Should you eat out at the same place regularly as part of research, then the Inland Revenue are liable to assess the individual, but the cost will usually be tax deductible for his employer.

5.   It is important to try out new competitive restaurants, or existing restaurants where they have changed the menu, in order to assess their impact on their market and also your own market. Hoteliers and restaurateurs can within reason charge this cost as a nominal business expense.

6.   Where the expenditure is on entertaining staff, a foreign customer, or research, then the VAT proportion can also be deductible as an input item for VAT, so you would save the current rate of VAT on the total bill and the balance would be deductible against your assessable profit.

7.   The cost of operating and subsidising staff restaurants and canteens (including directors' restaurants) is deductible for tax purposes. In practice, there will be occasions when outsiders are entertained in the same premises. But it is highly unlikely that the Inland Revenue would ask you to start sending them particulars of this in-house entertaining, and this tends to be 'lost' in the overall cost.

In practice it would be very difficult for you to estimate the actual cost of entertaining a small number of people in-house out of the total number of your employees and directors who are provided with restaurant facilities. However, some add-back of costs could be made in the taxation computation to cover this and thus forestall enquiries from the Inland Revenue.

*   *   *   *   *

The foregoing is a brief summary of some aspects of entertaining which are still deductible for tax purposes. Naturally, your own circumstances would have to be taken into account and I would strongly urge readers to discuss these points with their own tax advisers before drawing any conclusions.

15

Conclusion – A Different Attitude

On the whole subject of creating and sustaining goodwill and improving sales results there are numerous ways of making a successful impact on the market and many sales techniques to use.

One can achieve higher sales through paid advertising, unpaid publicity, sales letters, mailing shots, telephone sales calls and face-to-face selling. Most marketing experts will agree that at some stage the most important point is to get together in a face-to-face sales situation. It is probably the only sales technique where you can ask and answer questions, and watch for points on non-verbal communication – body language.

In successfully closing contracts (and indeed achieving higher sales generally) it is vital to try to get together in order to sell face-to-face, or what I call, eyeball-to-eyeball. It is very difficult to close without personal contact. Sometimes the face-to-face sales situation is in a factory or showroom examining or trying out the product. But very often the sales situation is not. What I am recommending is that on occasions this situation can be moved out of the office to a restaurant.

What could be more pleasant, in face-to-face selling, than to entertain. It is a good way to get to know your customer, find out how he ticks, try to get him to relax and establish a relationship with you so that he is far more receptive to the advantages of the product or service you are selling.

Apart from specific sales situations, business entertaining should be used more as a sales aid. Whatever your business and however pressured you are, there is a strong case for setting aside, say, one day a week for entertaining those customers and key contacts whom you do not necessarily meet very often.

Just think of the impact of entertaining 40 key contacts per year, in addition to those you entertain because they are with you that day. This could make a considerable impact on goodwill and sales. Why wait until you have to entertain an important client? Why not entertain as a planned exercise, just as successful executives plan mailing shots, sales letters and advertising?

The objective behind this book is simply to help you improve your results from business entertaining. All of the various points stressed are vitally important. But what is probably of greater importance is the attitude of mind I am trying to put across. This involves a significant amount of pre-planning and a continuous use of empathy. It also means getting the restaurant staff to, in a sense, become part of your sales force, by encouraging them to concentrate more on your guest than yourself.

There are around 200 key points in the previous chapters. Ten of the more important factors, in the form of Ten Commandments, are as follows:

Ten Commandments on Successful Business Entertaining

1. Successful business entertaining is significantly different to social entertaining.
2. Entertain in a restaurant you know well and where you are well known.
3. Always arrive there first.
4. Set objectives just as you would in any sales situation.
5. Large tips will not necessarily mean VIP treatment.
6. Waiters/waitresses are people and react positively to basic human relations treatment.
7. Make waiters part of your sales force.
8. Women executives have to 'educate' restaurants by persuasion not aggression.

9. Do *not* entertain your bank manager when you need an overdraft.

10. 'Stroke your buyer's ego' when you entertain.

Business entertaining done well can be a great investment. Just like paid advertising, mailing shots, it is a marketing cost. It is well nigh impossible to measure goodwill, and the improvement which can come from effective entertaining, but it can be substantial. I believe that after reading this book, you will be convinced that business entertaining should become one of the most important features of your marketing programme.